Diverging Time

The Politics of Modernity in Kant, Hegel, and Marx

David Carvounas

LEXINGTON BOOKS
Lanham • Boulder • New York • Oxford

LEXINGTON BOOKS

Published in the United States of America
by Lexington Books
An Imprint of the Rowman & Littlefield Publishing Group
4720 Boston Way, Lanham, Maryland 20706

12 Hid's Copse Road
Cumnor Hill, Oxford OX2 9JJ, England

British Library Cataloguing in Publication Information Available

Library of Congress Cataloging-in-Publication Data

Carvounas, David, 1964–
   Diverging time : the politics of modernity in Kant, Hegel, and
Marx / David Carvounas.
      p. cm.
Includes bibliographical references and index.
   ISBN 0-7391-0372-5 (alk. paper)—ISBN 0-7391-0373-3 (pbk. :
alk. paper)
   1. Time—Sociological aspects. 2. Civilization,
Modern—Philosophy. 3. Kant, Immanuel, 1724–1804—Contributions
in political science. 4. Hegel, Georg Wilhelm Friedrich,
1770–1831—Contributions in political science. 5. Marx, Karl,
1818–1883—Contributions in political science. I. Title.
   HM656 .C374 2002
   304.2'3—dc21

2002002165

Printed in the United States of America
⊖™ The paper used in this publication meets the minimum requirements of American
National Standard for Information Sciences—Permanence of Paper for Printed Library
Materials, ANSI/NISO Z39.48–1992.

For Alkis Kontos

Contents

Acknowledgments

I would like to give special thanks to an extraordinary teacher, Alkis Kontos, to whom this book is warmly dedicated, and to Graeme Nicholson, to whom I owe greatly for his kind intellectual support throughout the writing of the manuscript. I would also like to give thanks to Edward Andrew, Joseph Carens, Ronald Beiner, and Phillip Hansen for their helpful suggestions and observations on the manuscript. Thanks also to my colleague Craig Ireland, *fidus Achates*, whose unfailing critical assessment of the manuscript, from its inception to its completion, simply cannot be measured. Finally, I would like to thank Kristen Roberts for her patience and support.

Introduction

In his preface to the twelfth edition of *Democracy in America*, Alexis de Tocqueville tells us that when he wrote this study in 1835 his mind was singularly occupied: every page has a "solemn warning" that the form of society is changing, and that the conditions under which humanity lives are changing, and that as a consequence "new destinies are impending."[1] Tocqueville does not exaggerate; however, since his warnings surely come too late for us today, they are to a certain extent less apposite. More important are some of the consequences that he observes in the world around him, consequences which he attributes at least in part to a *new* guiding ethos of humanity. Tocqueville finds an example of this ethos when he asks an American sailor "why the ships of his country are built so as to last but for a short time." Without reflecting for a moment the sailor answers that the "art of navigation is every day making such rapid progress, that the finest vessel would become almost useless if it lasted beyond a certain number of years." With this response, Tocqueville recognizes the "idea upon which a great people directs all its concerns."[2] All concerns are directed toward a present that is known to be transitory, and a future that is expected to be different from, and better than, the past. Tocqueville knows that many consequences follow from this idea, and while he is underwhelmed by the apparent effect this ethos has had on the *present* culture of the Americans who espouse it, he confesses that he is overwhelmed by the task of identifying its possible *future* consequences for humanity as a whole. New destinies are indeed forthcoming, but in looking over the changing social, political, and cultural landscape of the modern world, Tocqueville can only remark that

> the world which is rising into existence is still half encumbered by the remains of the world which is waning into decay; and amidst the vast perplexity of human affairs, none can say how much of ancient institutions and former manners will remain, or how much will completely disappear. Although the revolution which

is taking place in the social condition, the laws, the opinions, and the feelings of men, is still very far from being terminated, yet its results already admit of no comparison with anything that the world has ever before witnessed.[3]

Without a hint of nostalgia Tocqueville concludes his study by offering not a simple warning, but instead a remarkable observation: "I go back from age to age up to the remotest antiquity; but I find no parallel to what is occurring before my eyes: as the past has ceased to throw its light upon the future, the mind of man wanders in obscurity."[4] This is not an *indictment* of modernity which stubbornly refuses to see the light from the past; it is instead an insight into a *predicament* in which humanity finds itself at an early stage of modernity.

The predicament to which Tocqueville alludes is that modernity cannot depend on the light from the past to illuminate its future. Without a source of light, the future becomes cloaked in darkness and the present lacks the vision to move forward. The modern mind of the present, as if in a dark wood, wanders in obscurity. But the modern mind did not wander in obscurity for long, if at all. Tocqueville strained his eyes looking for light from previous ages and found nothing to illuminate the changes taking place around him; but he was looking in the wrong place, or the wrong time. He does not behold the light emanating from the future itself. Tocqueville was correct: the past had ceased to shine its light upon the future; but while the modern present required light to journey forward, it did not need light from the past, because the future had its own source of light, a source fueled by human imagination. This new light, shining brilliantly, illuminates things that were hitherto concealed in the shadows of human existence. With this light emerges a new awareness not only of the world that exists but of a world that can be created. The modern present burns with expectations of a better life—a new life that is just on the horizon. The modern world could move confidently toward this light, leaving the past behind.

The predicament of modernity, however, is more complicated. It discloses the more serious problem of temporal coordination encountered by modernity; a problem that for centuries was concealed by the dominance of the past over the present and future. Before the modern age, a ubiquitous past held sway over both present and future, thus giving temporality its general coherence. Once the past could no longer perform this role, a new way to coordinate the modes of time became imperative. And it was to the future that modernity turned for this subtle yet demanding task. Replacing a past orientation with a future orientation posed risks; a past orientation had offered humanity a well-traveled path with time-honored experiences, while a future orientation could at best offer humanity a new journey with expectations of a better life. Yet the coordination of time with light from the future seemed worth the risk. Besides, replacing light from the past with light from the future had the advantage not only of providing temporal coordination but also of illuminating a new political vision. In fact, modern temporal coordination is impossible without a political vision of a better future.

The three most imaginative and fundamental moments depicting modern attempts to reconcile the modes of time, while simultaneously providing humanity with a new political vision, are found in the political thought of Immanuel Kant, Georg Wilhelm Friedrich Hegel, and Karl Marx. Kant gives expression to the Enlightenment by offering humanity the hope of progress. The modern age may not yet be an enlightened one, but humanity shows unmistakable signs of emerging from its self-imposed immaturity. To hasten this emergence and to guide humanity forward, Kant looks not to the exemplary nature of past wisdom and truth, but instead to faith in the wisdom and truth of progress—a faith that couples a cautious optimism in future improvement with rationality and future-oriented activity. The idea of progress is for Kant the link that connects the modern present with the recently undermined past, and the modern present with the yet-to-be *created* future. Whereas Kant offers the hope of progress, Hegel offers a theory of historical time. Understanding the dynamics of historical time gives the modern world a way to make intelligible the proliferation of the *new* that became a salient feature of modernity. Hegel's theory of historical time uncovers continuity among change, which both facilitates the reconstruction of a coherent past and illuminates the features of approaching change, thereby bridging an increasingly disjunctive past and future. For Hegel the past is viewed as a theater where historical change involves the dissolution of the old and the rise of the new, and this not so much at the expense of the past than as a necessary and logical product of the past. By attempting to recapture the spirit of the past, thus connecting the modern present to what preceded it, Hegel makes a strong, *modern* case that the past is politically and logically unretrievable, and that a genuinely *new* future is emerging. The modern present, and its *immediate future*, however, is as far as Hegel's philosophy can take us. As Marx sees it, Hegel's philosophy takes us a long way, but not quite far enough. Marx is a political philosopher who demands that the world be changed and not just interpreted, but he is also a historian who understands that while humans can make history, they do not make it under conditions of their own choosing. The past thus exercises an influence on the present and circumscribes choices for the creation of something totally new. Marx tells us that human emancipation is on the horizon, and that a radical future orientation is necessary, but we cannot just leap into the future; we must instead act upon the future-potential in the present.

Kant, Hegel, and Marx felt they were providing humanity with the vision necessary to journey forward into the modern age, visions which include new interpretations of the past, present, and future, and new ways of conjoining them. But looking back over the last couple of centuries is it hard not to notice that the journey toward a better future has proven to be difficult if not altogether elusive. It is even harder not to notice that grand visions of a better future seem to have given way to the exigencies of the immediate present. Dominated by short-term concerns of daily life, we find our expectations diminishing and our orientation toward the future more difficult to maintain. With diminishing expectations, the future appears far less resplendent today than it did two centuries ago; and as a result, we advance into a new millennium with a dimly lit horizon. Perhaps what Tocqueville said about the past ceasing to throw its light can now be said about the future. But without light from either the past or the future, his observation that the modern mind wanders in obscurity is even more appropriate today than it was some two centuries ago. Hence, if a disjunctive past and future gave birth to modernity, and if modernity required a new way to bridge this disjunction, then the new, modern way to coordinate temporality seems today to have lost its coherence. The problem of temporal coordination seems to have returned, but with this crucial difference: we are now more removed from our past yet at the same time less enthusiastic about the prospect of creating a new future.

If this book returns to the beginning of the modern age, or to the emergence of a temporality *specific to modernity*, it is neither to satiate idle fantasy, nor to fashion a study confined to the history of ideas; it returns instead to show how Kant, Hegel, and Marx strategically contribute to our understanding of the meaning of modernity from their particular position within the perspective of temporality. This particular perspective does not intend to challenge or eclipse other perspectives, but may provide a context, *modern temporality*, within which other perspectives may be located. More important, this book argues that this perspective is necessary to understand our current rapport, or lack thereof, with the future. By returning to the advent of modernity—when a once ubiquitous past orientation gives way to an ascending future orientation—this book considers the future *of* modernity by exploring the future *in* modernity. This maneuver is important because whether modernity has a future is very much tied up with the extent to which it can both maintain the idea of an open future, and provide an orientation to the future in terms of new expectations and possibilities.

Notes

1. Alexis de Tocqueville, "Author's Preface to the Twelfth Edition," in *Democracy in America*, trans. Henry Reeve, revised by Francis Bowen, vol. 1 (New York: Vintage Books, 1945), ix.

2. Tocqueville, *Democracy in America*, vol. 2, 35.

3. Tocqueville, *Democracy in America*, 349.

4. Tocqueville, *Democracy in America*, 349.

Chapter One

Modernity and the Future as a Problem

Modernity, Time, and Temporality

Modernity has recently become a central theme for political and social thought, and the literature on modernity has been multiplying accordingly. Since the early 1980s, studies of modernity have proliferated at the same pace as its supposed displacement by the postmodern age—apparently confirming Hegel's adage of the owl of Minerva spreading its wings only at dusk. Modernity is considered normally along with the two closely related moments of modernization and modernism—yet the boundaries between these three moments are not easily discernible. Modernization often refers to scientific and technological advances and to processes of secularization, individualization, urbanization, industrialization, commodification, and bureaucratization. Such developments are marked by changes in individual and social relations, relations between classes, relations between individuals and machines, and between individuals and the objects of economic production. Modernism is the aesthetic-artistic reflection upon, and the cultural response to and critique of, the processes and effects of modernization. Modernism emerged in inchoate form toward the end of the nineteenth century, and congealed into often rebellious avant-garde movements early in the twentieth century.

Modernity has been increasingly disengaged from these closely related moments and has become the preferred object of study. Broadly speaking, those who deal with modernity invariably seek to examine the individual, social, and experiential condition under the changed circumstances that ensued from the modern processes of secularization, individualization, urbanization, and industrialization. Accordingly, many perceptive studies have characterized modernity, inter alia, as that which is dynamic, ephemeral, and transitory, or as a disenchanted world coupled with a generalized loss of meaning, or as the dominance of instrumental rationality, or even as a secularized eschatology.[1] While there are many possible vantage points from which to consider modernity, it appears that time and temporality constitute a crucial common denominator. Most theories of modernity attempt to circumscribe the specificity of the modern by sharply demarcating it from the premodern. As such, modernity is a term designating a particular period, epoch, or *time* in history. In conceiving itself as an epoch, no doubt modernity created past epochs; nevertheless, beginning with the Renaissance but finding full expression during the Enlightenment, modernity asserted itself as an unprecedented and radically new epoch.

Modernity in this epochal sense, as a distinct period *in* time, is however less the focus of this study than is the apparent epochal change in time consciousness. Focused attention and interpretation are given to what emerged as a new form of temporality—the manner by which past, present, and future are coordinated—or better yet, to a specifically modern temporality which decisively changed our orientation or *relationship to the future*.[2] Of course, we must be cautious in depicting the emergence of modernity and its new form of time consciousness as some kind of historical rupture if only because, as Peter Wagner explains, notions such as *rupture* and *revolutionary events* normally refer to the changed orientations of a relative few, and "if modernity was to mark a condition or experience, then the qualifications required to show its existence were largely absent in the allegedly modern societies during the nineteenth century, and for a still fairly large number of people during the first half of the twentieth century."[3] While maybe not a historical rupture which suddenly ensnared a hapless population, it is fair to say that for the last two hundred years many have been either enticed or forced out of premodern forms of temporality and sociability and into the project of modernity—a project that has been *increasingly distinguishing* itself from the premodern precisely by the diminishing use of the exemplary status of past experience, and by its unique rapport with the future. Moreover, it is important to keep in mind that if this study contends that temporality is a crucial component of modernity, it does not maintain that modernity is definable exclusively through the specificity of its temporality; it contends instead that temporality is that without which modernity cannot be fully understood or, if you will, that temporality is a necessary, though not necessarily a sufficient, condition of possibility for the understanding of modernity.

To better understand this peculiarly modern temporality, we turn to Reinhart Koselleck's studies on the semantics of historical time because he *historicizes* the relationship between the past, present, and future, which helps to expose a temporality specific to modernity.[4] Koselleck tells us that for more than two thousand years history was "presented as a kind of reservoir of multiplied experiences which the readers can learn and make their own" and the idiom *historia magistra vitae* persisted until the eighteenth century, at which point it gradually dissolved within and was eventually replaced by the modern concept of historical process.[5] The dethroning of the old topos of *historia magistra vitae* decisively changed the relation between past and future. The possibility of thinking that the future could be different from the past, Koselleck tells us, occurred when the concept of history itself shifted from an experiential continuity, which allowed *histories* to serve as an exemplar of life's teachings, to *history* as part of a temporal process that singularizes past phenomena into unique events that need not hold exemplary force. What is important in the present context is the emergence of a peculiarly modern topos, and not Koselleck's contention that the shifting semantic relations ultimately led to the breakup of the old topos. Koselleck tells us that "it was the philosophy of historical process which first detached early modernity from its past and at the same time inaugurated our modernity with a new future."[6] By relying on a presupposed similitude of circumstances and an assumed trans-temporal subjectivity or experiential similitude, the premodern topos could but yield a very circumscribed orientation toward the future. However, by the late eighteenth century the past was increasingly perceived as a process of unique, nonreproducible events, and this in turn permitted the future to be conceived as potentially different from the past.[7] It is here that a specifically modern temporality can be distinguished from its premodern homologue, a modern temporality with a distinctly modern rapport with the future.

In considering the changing relation between past and future, and in demarcating modern temporality from its premodern homologue, Koselleck seeks to disclose the variations of historical time and the temporal structure of historical experience. In doing so, Koselleck uses the metahistorical categories of space of experience (*Erfahrungsraum*) and horizon of expectation (*Erwartungshorizont*) to help "deduce the shifting classification of experience and expectation," thereby allowing for the demonstration of how historical time alters with history.[8] What is important here is not whether these categories are indeed anthropological constants which establish the conditions of possible histories;[9] what is important is instead the changed relation between past and future with the advent of modernity—a relation that Koselleck uncovers using the categories of space of experience and horizon of expectation. As noted above, prior to the changed experiential condition that was opened up by the emergence of modernity, the horizon of expectation of the ancient and medieval world was limited by past experiences. The old topos relied on a continuity of circumstances that would reinforce the validity of past experience to bind expectations. With the arrival of modernity and the ability of the past to inform the present increasingly becoming more and more insignificant, and with the emergence of corresponding expectations that the future will be different from the past, the present stands as a transition to something new. With the past thus foreshortened, the future could not but accelerate, unbridled, and, to defer once again to Koselleck, the "divide between previous experience and coming expectation opened up, and the difference between past and present increased, so that lived time was experienced as a rupture, as a period of transition in which the new and the unexpected continually happened."[10]

What we learn from Koselleck is not only a viable account of the transition period demarcating the premodern era from the modern age, but also the historical nature of temporality, or more specifically, the historicity of the future. Temporal-ity, or the way in which past, present, and future are coordinated, is subject to historical change. It is this latter point that is of import for us. Indeed, before the modern age, past, present, and future were essentially experientially contiguous with a past holding sway over the present and future. This contiguity provided temporal coherence by furnishing experientially validated meaning to a present which remains in continuity with an already articulated future. When this specifically historical temporality lost its grounding in the past, as it seems to have done with the advent of modernity, the present and especially the future were loosened from their moorings and temporality lost its general coherence. It is this temporal discontinuity which becomes a problem for modernity—a problem which demanded ways to bridge the rupture between past and present, or qualitatively different ways in which to coordinate the modalities of time. One such way, which is the focus of this study, has been to coordinate the modes of time through an orientation toward the future.

To understand better the significance of this temporal shift, as well as to explain better the historical nature of the future, we should explore briefly the nature of past notions of futurity. Exaggeration is always a risk when presenting a rudimentary diachronic sketch of such a complex phenomenon; however, an excursion into past notions of futurity, and into the writings of some ancient and medieval thinkers, is necessary to grasp the various ways in which the past could inform and restrict future orientation.[11]

Excursus into Past Notions of Futurity

Holding the view that the future did not surface as a problem until the modern age does not imply that the ancient and medieval worlds lacked a future orientation or a distinction between past, present, and future.[12] Such a view, however, can suggest a contrast regarding their relationship or rapport with the future. Modern futurity can be characterized as a specific future orientation relatively unencumbered by what it sees as a transitory and largely supersedable past. In contrast, ancient and medieval futurity can be characterized by either a future orientation that was held at bay by an enduring, instructive, and authoritative past, or a future orientation reined in by the influence of Christian eschatology, or both simultaneously. Premodern temporality, in other words, envisions the future less at the expense of the past than in terms of the past, or in terms of an atemporal present. For example, in his study of the temporal dynamics which distinguish the ancient epic from the modern novel, M. M. Bakhtin writes that

> the world of the epic is the national heroic past; it is a world of "beginnings" and "peak times" in the national history, a world of fathers and of founders of families, a world of "firsts" and "bests." The important point here is not that the past constitutes the content of the epic. The formally constitutive feature of the

epic as a genre is rather the transferral of a represented world into the past, and the degree to which this world participates in the past.[13]

Located in what Bakhtin describes as an *absolute past*, the epic world is a complete, self-contained whole which is preserved and revealed as tradition. Handed down and conferred as tradition, it eschews new insights and personal initiative in its interpretation, and demands instead a pious attitude toward it and a uniform and common interpretation.[14] The important point to emphasize is that this "absolute past" of the epic is predominantly an evaluating category. The central categories of *first, founder, beginning*, and the like are not just temporal indicators, but rather, as Bakhtin rightly argues, valorized temporal categories: "In the past, everything is good: all the really good things (i.e., the 'first' things) occur only in this past. The epic absolute past is the single source and beginning of everything good for all later times as well."[15] This temporal hierarchy places notions such as perfection and harmony in the past, and is characterized by a distinctive concept of time, especially future-time. Since all ideals are shifted to the past or into a fanciful present, the present and chiefly the past are valorized while the future is emptied of any real substance. Authenticity, in other words, requires a previous existence in some *natural state* or in some *golden age*. Moreover, concomitant with this inversion is a "greater readiness to build a superstructure for reality (the present) along a vertical axis of upper and lower than to move forward along the horizontal axis of time."[16]

This epic time and its corresponding temporal hierarchy are not limited to mythological and cultural-artistic modes of expression, but also form and inform ancient political philosophy. Plato's eternal and pregiven Forms, for instance, are such that nothing *new* enters the world. Reluctantly dragged into the historical-temporal world of politics, Plato, in the *Republic*, designs a polis with reference to a divine model whereby the philosophers look "back and forth to Justice, Beauty, Moderation, and all such things as by nature exist . . . basing their judgment on what Homer too called the divine and godlike existing in man."[17] Plato's ideal is certainly not utopian in the modern sense.[18] This is true not only because it lacks the characteristically modern aspect of prospective vision or a movement from the present into a newly wrought future, but also because Plato's ideal polis simply cannot endure an extended future. Imitating the epic style of Homer, Plato defers the question about the future of the ideal polis to the Muses. The ideal polis, if brought about, becomes part of the inevitable cycle of growth and dissolution: The Muses express it this way:

> It is hard for a city composed in this way to change. But everything that is born must perish. Not even a constitution such as this will last forever but it must face dissolution, and its dissolution will be as follows. Not only all plants which grow in the earth but all animals which grow upon it have periods of birth and

barrenness of both soul and body whenever the cycles of their existence complete the circumference of their circles.[19]

The Muses tell a story of what *will* occur—not as a prophesy but what must occur according to the logic of natural decay. The future is already charted out, already articulated and contained within the inevitable cycle of growth and dissolution. Here there is no room for human intervention to avert inescapable dissolution in their own far-off future, the *first* and *last* words have been spoken. Moreover, the cycle of political change is neither chaotic nor unknowable, but instead a mathematically calculable affair.

Such a uniform direction strikes Aristotle as too simplistic a way of under-standing political change and revolution.[20] Aristotle eschews a singular-cyclical pattern while setting forth a theory of political change which respects its sometimes unpredictable nature.[21] Yet, while Aristotle quibbles over the singular-cyclical pattern of Plato's theory of political change, the scope of possible change or the actual permutations are for Aristotle still delimited. While not unidirectional, neither is it developmental or temporally linear. Aristotle does not entertain the possibility of development toward a completely new regime or even the possibility of future development in general. This highlights a specific characteristic of ancient political thought; as M. I. Finley explains, there is a certain "absence in antiquity of any idea of a forward-looking, progressive change in the political or social structure," and ancient revolutions were "not mere jacqueries, but they were also not ventures into the future."[22] To be sure, one may wish to depart theoretically from the delimitation of common experience and past wisdom; however, as Aristotle sees it, by searching for something *new* one overlooks the fact that "it is necessary to pay attention to the length of time and the many years during which it would not have escaped notice if this condition were a fine one; *for nearly everything has been discovered*, though some things have not been brought together, while others are known but not practised."[23] According to this, what is possible is limited by what already exists or what already is known to have existed. Within this kaleidoscope of changeless change, Aristotle does acknowledge a discernible development up to his own time; he just does not entertain the possibility of any future development in the fundamental order of things. The constancy of human experience, which serves as a guide to human nature, binds future expectations and limits the horizon of the political. There is a sense of irony here in that even with his keen empirical insight into politics, Aristotle has no sense of the epochal change that was taking place around him. There is no hint in his writing, for example, that, as A. C. Bradley writes, Greek civilization was "something transitory, or a single stage in history. Though he had been tutor to Alexander, he seems unaware that the day of autonomous republics was passing, and that in the Macedonian monarch a kind of government was arising *hitherto unknown* in the development of his race."[24]

A fundamental transformation in the attitude toward the future did, however, take place within the Christian era. "The medieval world's relation to time," writes Helmut Plesner, "was defined by the Church's transcendence of time." And since "truth is materially secure, as a store of supernatural revelation or as laws of being which are immanent to reason, the successive clarification of which in the course of enquiry is part of a closed order which is given once and for all."[25] Within this closed order a shift in the idea of time and history occurred whereby the ancient understanding of the past gave way to an understanding of the past predicated on a belief in creation.[26] The Christian belief in a world created by God gave the world a precise beginning and a determinate end (which God has assigned) as well as a present conceived as an elemental part of this sequence. The historic past is thereby understood universally in terms of everything having its place in the Divine plan, as Saint Augustine tells us, "the right education of that part of the human race which consists of the people of God has, like that of a single man, advanced through certain epochs or, as it were, ages, so that it might rise upwards from temporal to eternal things, and from the visible to the invisible."[27]

This development of the human race is seen in the light of God's plan as laid out in Scripture, and the epochs are therefore religious epochs. The details of these epochs need not detain us here;[28] we need only pause to consider Augustine's attitude toward the events of earthly history as well as the termination of history itself. First, for Augustine it is clear that in the temporal space between the radically *unique* historical event of the appearance of Christ and the impending Last Judgment, history is nothing but the history of faith and unbelief. Augustine is eager to point out that historical events, such as the fall of the Roman Empire, can in no way be seen as either instruments of, or as obstacles to, salvation.[29] The struggle between faith and unbelief, therefore, has nothing to do with the actual trajectory of historical development.[30] Second, Augustine is a theologian, not a historian. Theologically speaking, history has a trajectory without discernible movement, and in this sense, the future is not a continuation of the historical process, but the termination of it. Moreover, in this theological view of history, as Erich Auerbach explains,

> the individual earthly event is not regarded as a definitive self-sufficient reality, nor as a link in a chain of development in which single events or combinations of events perpetually give rise to new events, but viewed primarily in immediate vertical connection with a divine order which encompasses it, which on some future day will itself be concrete reality; so that the earthly event is a prophecy or figura of a part of a wholly divine reality that will be enacted in the future; it is always present in the eye of God and in the other world, which is to say that in transcendence the revealed and true reality is present at all times, or timelessly.[31]

From this perspective, the future has happened already, since the horizontal flow of time is vertically connected to Divine Providence. From the more mundane perspective of the historical flow of individual life, a future radically different from the past is predicated upon a future unhinged from the historical process and placed beyond the grasp of human action. Thus, for all its emphasis on a future redemption, the future orientation characteristic of eschatology is not of the same order as the future orientation characteristic of modernity. In contrast to the future orientation of modernity, the future orientation of eschatology is no less circumscribed than the futurity of the ancients. What is more, in a section on the *hidden time* of the end of the world, Augustine remarks that many try in vain to "compute and define the number of years that remain for this world, since we hear from the mouth of Truth himself that it is not for us to know this."[32] Strictly speaking, therefore, the future is not our concern. Of course, this position leaves out the likes of Joachim of Fiore and Thomas Müntzer, and countless lesser known individuals, who believed in a more revolutionary Christ—not to mention the chiliastic and millenarian movements that worshiped a Christ who taught not that heaven will come to earth, but instead that earth must be transformed into a heaven. However, these beliefs were condemned as heretical by the more conservative Christian church, which agreed with Augustine that the creation of a radically new future is best left to God.[33] Until the time of the divinely enacted future, the earthly city must rely on the wisdom of the past so long as it is sufficiently Christianized: statements by pagan philosophers, writes Augustine, "which happen to be true and consistent with our faith should not cause alarm, but be claimed for our own use, as it were from owners who have no right to them."[34]

The Augustinian commingling of the ancient tradition with that of Holy Scripture (buttressed, of course, by a Romanized Church) became the favored approach to political philosophy for the next thousand years. Considering themselves direct heirs of classical Greece and Rome, medieval political philosophers adapted the lessons of the past to their own present circumstances.[35] The way in which the past was used to inform the present and thus to help contain futurity can best be seen in the *mirror of princes* genre. This genre of political writing is aptly named since it reflects sight to what is behind (the past) and not to what is ahead (the future). Essentially a conventionalized way of establishing one's erudition, these mirrors were largely instruction manuals or advice books, written by university-trained intellectuals, intended to inform kings about the nature of good government, on how kings differ from tyrants, on the duties of good rulers, and offering moral instruction and examples of good rulership from antiquity and especially the judges and kings of the Old Testament.[36] Such political writings, informed as they were by the wisdom of the past and placed within the context of salvational history, did not view the future as a *special* problem. With nothing new expected to arise (at least not until the *Parousia*), and with the present always already articulated and buttressed by the transcendental order of things, the future did not need to be considered as a special problem.

Such a perspective is quite commonplace as late as Desiderius Erasmus[37] and even as late as the supposed modern thinker Niccolò Machiavelli. Indeed, characteristic of this medieval genre, Machiavelli's *Discourses* instruct us that "anyone wishing to see what is to come should examine what has been, for all the affairs of the world in every age have had their counterparts in ancient times." This is predicated upon a constancy of human nature in that for Machiavelli the affairs of the world are "carried on by men who have, and have always had, the same passions, and of necessity, the same results come from them."[38] Further, in *The Prince* he writes, "a prudent man should always enter upon the paths beaten by great men, and imitate those who have been most excellent."[39] Of course, characteristic of Renaissance thought Machiavelli recognizes the importance of free will, of securing one's own destiny, but this represents a hill rather than a mountain of thought. His conception of free will (a forward glance) is also shackled by a past yet to be thrown off (antiquity). The authoritative nature of the past allows for the imitation of its successes and the avoidance of its mistakes, and one may become a prudent ruler only by learning the lessons history has to offer. With this view of history, Machiavelli expounds a view of politics according to which the experience of the past can be used by present political actors to create a future that can be as glorious as, but essentially no different from, the past.

Not until the political thought of Thomas Hobbes do we find a discernible shift in the attitude toward the past and the future. Hobbes does for modern political philosophy what Bacon, who looked upon inherited scientific knowledge as wrongfully sacrosanct, does for modern science, and what Descartes, who rejected preconceived notions by wrapping himself in a cocoon of doubt thus severing himself from the past and the future, does for modern philosophy. By questioning the value of past political experience and the philosophical principles upon which previous political societies had been established, Hobbes gives us the first modern glimpse into the way in which the past can be displaced or superseded. We must remember that Hobbes is writing in a world where the old social, economic, and political structures of medieval society had all but collapsed, and where the Religious Peace of Augsburg (1555) had all but replaced the grand, universal claims of religion with the principle of *cuius regio, eius religio*. Eugene Weber summarizes this early modern period best as a

> search for structure, or, rather, many different quests to renew or replace the structures of a world that had become much broader, more complex, more confused; a world in which the reassuring routines of worship, habit, and social groups had broken down; [and where] social groups had changed their function, states had grown, economies had altered, units had broken down and other units formed. Change had wrought confusion—of place and duties, of authority, of who did what and how and by what right. The late sixteenth and seventeenth centuries seem, in overview, to be devoted to a reordering task, the forging of attitudes and institutions—political and religious, social and mental—which would bring some means of control in this new-wrought world.[40]

Hobbes argues for the creation of a *new* political order buttressed by the mechanical laws recently uncovered by the new natural sciences—which, while still in their infancy, were radically recasting human understanding of the natural world.[41] Hobbes saw himself as the originator of a new political philosophy: "Natural Philosophy is therefore but young; but Civil Philosophy yet much younger, as being no older . . . than my own book *De Cive*."[42] Introducing the mechanical laws of natural science into human psychology and politics, he outlines a new science of political society which provides the knowledge necessary, if applied, for the creation of an artificial political society.[43] Holding such a view has important consequences for the way in which both the past and the future are articulated. Hobbes's political philosophy, based on the understanding of the mechanical laws which govern all reality, need not take into consideration previous political experience or the teachings of the historical past. Methodologically speaking, past social and political history, and its supposed exemplary nature, can be either dispensed with completely or cataloged as a series of false attempts at establishing political society; likewise with past political philosophy, which can be rejected as lacking the effective knowledge necessary to achieve a stable political order. Political philosophers, in other words, need not look to human history in order to understand how human beings act or unite themselves into a political order any more than natural scientists need to study the history of an atom to understand the mechanical laws under which it acts. Armed with the scientific knowledge that human beings are but matter in motion conforming to the same simple mechanical laws that govern the motion of all matter, abstraction from all social relations (both past and present) is possible. In this hypothetical state of nature, individuals are without historical, religious, or ethical roots, without customs or traditions; in short, the past is detached from all historical constructions and demoted from its instructive and authoritative status.[44] The past that remains can be understood abstractly as one of war and pseudo peace from which Hobbes offers an escape—an escape which can be characterized as exchanging a past for a *new* future.

To be sure, unlike much of modern political philosophy that follows him, Hobbes does not offer a grand transformative vision—there is neither a theory of historical development, nor a theory of historical progress, nor even a theory which seeks to transform human nature. Yet, what makes Hobbes more of a modern when compared to his predecessors is that by summarily dismissing any assistance from the past, the future (or future orientation) becomes the predominant motif in his political philosophy. For instance, Hobbes bases much of his theory of human nature on the *voluntary motion* of desire, which is an *anticipatory* emotion; power is defined as the "present means to obtain some future apparent Good";[45] felicity is the *continual success* in acquiring the objects of desire,[46] which, in turn, is a felicity in this life and consisteth not in the repose of a mind satisfied. For there is no such Finis ultimus, (utmost ayme), nor Summum Bonum (greatest good), as is spoken of in the Books of the old Morall Philosophers. Nor can a man any more live, whose Desires are at an end, than he, whose Senses and Imagination are at a stand. Felicity is a continuall progresse of the desire, from one object to another; the attaining of the former, being still but the way to the later. The cause whereof is, That the object of mans desire, is not to enjoy once onely, and for one instant of time; but to assure for ever, the way of his future desire. And therefore the voluntary actions, and inclinations of all men, tend, not only to the procuring, but also to the assuring of a contented life.[47]

This specific secular and materialistic rapport with the future requires provident individuals; however, without a stable social and political order in the present, an individual who looks ahead "in care of future time, hath his heart all the day long, gnawed on by feare of death, poverty, or other calamity; and has no repose, nor pause of his anxiety, but in sleep."[48] Of course, the context in which this passage is found is Hobbes's view on the natural origins of religion (anxiety of time to come); but, it is certainly not a stretch to see its continued relevance (or return) in a secular, materialist worldview. Hobbes, as one of the first moderns to theoretically confront a future detached from its reliance on the past, perceives that much fear and anxiety are associated with both this detachment and the subsequent need for assuring a contented future *in this life*. Hobbes's political philosophy, therefore, attempts to help master or tame this modern anxiety about the future by securing the present (by establishing a strong sovereign power), thereby giving a rational hope for a contented life in the future. While he does put forward a scientific model of political order that is static and relatively unchanging, such a model is still predicated on future-oriented individuals. Hobbes is clearly the first modern in this respect.

Futurity and Modern Political Philosophy

While premodern societies were not entirely bereft of a future orientation or of the capacity for distinguishing between past, present, and future, such societies nevertheless held the future at bay. The future was to a large extent held in check by the sheer weight of traditions and by past experiences in general. Or, as Koselleck would have it, the horizon of expectations of premodern society were so circumscribed by tradition and past experiences that expectations "subsisted entirely on the experiences of their predecessors, experiences which in turn became those of the successors," and change was so *imperceptible* that the "rent between previous experience and an expectation to be newly disclosed did not undermine the traditional world."[49] The past furnished the present and the future with a general sense of continuity, meaning, and purpose; and most important, it provided political philosophers with a strict but coherent political boundary. Nevertheless, since the way in which past, present, and future are coordinated is not exempt from the vicissitudes of historical change, this state of affairs could not withstand, at the very least, the gradual transition of a vertically and hierarchically stratified society into a society horizontally and functionally differentiated into interdependent subsystems. The sociohistorical vectors behind the transition from a predominantly agrarian economy to one based increasingly on industry and manufacture are a long and well-known story and need not detain us here. Suffice it to say that the general dynamic involved was one in which the consolidation of networks of horizontal dependencies (i.e., the intensified circulation of exchangeable commodities) could no longer be accommodated by the vertical relationships of dependence character-istic of a feudal socioeconomic system based on self-sufficient and regional economic units.[50] These developments, along with various changes that were taking place in scientific knowledge, in forms of worship and religious cosmologies, in local and kinship ties, and in political institutions, helped to usher in a world with no parallel in the past.[51] The result became evident to the astute early-nineteenth-century observer Tocqueville, who perceived a temporal shift taking place—the past had indeed ceased to shine its light upon the future.

The modern world needed a new source or a new kind of light to provide the present with a general sense of continuity, meaning, and purpose. If the past could no longer provide the light, then the future would have to provide it, and with this light came a new political vision. With the emergence of modern temporality, future possibilities were no longer hemmed in by traditions or shackled by the past. Once past experience no longer tethered expectations, envisioning a future decidedly different from the past became possible. With the birth of modernity the past became undermined and the future valorized to such a degree that temporality became dominated by an open future rather than one delimited in advance by past practices or orientations. While modernity faced a future that was open, or at least viewed as being unfettered by the past, it also faced the problem of temporal coordination. This is to say that when the past appeared distant from rather than seamlessly continuous with the present, the past and tradition lost their grip on the present, and the need for temporal continuity became acute. The disjunction between the past and future demanded a new, modern conjunction of past, present, and future. The future, which is no longer prearticulated according to tradition or circumscribed in terms of the past, becomes in the modern age the focal point for a new organizing principle or transcendental anchor. As the past and present are henceforth coordinated with reference to the future, the weight of the past or tradition shifts accordingly to the future. The arrival of modernity and the dislodging of future orientation from its reliance on past experiences, therefore, required a shift to occur in the trend and substance of political philosophy. Subsequent and predominant trends in modern political philosophy valorized the future, demoted the past, and placed humans in the role of potential authors of a yet-to-be scripted future. This in turn enabled the assimilation of new experiences, while enabling the construction of new individual and social identities through an orientation toward the future.

It is no doubt true that with the rift between past and future, memory and hope, experience and expectation, and with the eclipse of a prearticulated and circumscribed future, the modern mind wanders in obscurity. Indeed, many have rightly characterized modern experience as fragmented and ephemeral; yet beneath this (or because of this) lies the need, desire, or hope that *incipit vita nova*, and the forging of new narratives connecting the modes of time helped to solidify this hope. While the hope for a new life is as old as it is new, it attains the force and a horizon in which it can be articulated *only* with the birth of modernity and its new rapport with the future. The three chapters that follow have as their focus this changed rapport with the future. Each chapter examines various attempts to mend the rift between past and future; and coordinating temporality with a greater emphasis on the future helped to make sense of the newness characteristic of the modern age, and to facilitate the birth of a truly new life for humanity.

Notes

1. Examples of various perspectives on modernity are Marshall Berman, *All That is Solid Melts into Air* (New York: Simon & Schuster, 1982); Hans Blumenberg, *The Legitimacy of the Modern Age*, trans. Robert M. Wallace (Cambridge, Mass.: MIT Press, 1983); David Frisby, *Fragments of Modernity* (Cambridge, Mass.: MIT Press, 1986); Jürgen Habermas, *The Philosophical Discourse of Modernity*, trans. Frederick G. Lawrence (Cambridge, Mass.: MIT Press, 1987); Matei Calinescu, *Five Faces of Modernity* (Durham, N.C.: Duke University Press, 1987); Anthony Giddens, *The Consequences of Modernity* (Stanford, Calif.: Stanford University Press, 1990) and *Modernity and Self-Identity* (Stanford, Calif.: Stanford University Press, 1991); William E. Connolly, *Political Theory and Modernity* (Oxford: Basil Blackwell, 1998); Louis Dupré, *Passage to Modernity* (New Haven, Conn.: Yale University Press, 1993); Peter Wagner, *A Sociology of Modernity* (New York: Routledge, 1994).

2. Temporality is hereby used in the *historical* and not the *transcendental* sense of the word. Transcendentally, every person, society, and epoch lived (or lives) temporally, thus with *a* past, present, and future. But this study speaks of past, present, and future in the historical sense, thus of *our past* (or *the* past), *our present* or *our future* (or *the* present and future). Furthermore, *time* in the sense of duration or clock-time or time measurement, while also indicators of modernity, will not be entertained in this study. For historical considerations of time in this sense see E. P. Thompson's famous essay "Time, Work-Discipline, and Industrial Capitalism," *Past and Present*, no. 38 (1967), 56–97. For more recent studies see Arno Borst's *The Ordering of Time: From the Ancient Computus to the Modern Computer*, trans. Andrew Winnard (Chicago: University of Chicago Press, 1993), and Gerhard Dohrn-Van Rossum's *History of the Hour: Clocks and Modern Temporal Orders*, trans. Thomas Dunlap (Chicago: University of Chicago Press, 1996).

3. Wagner, *A Sociology of Modernity* (New York: Routledge, 1994), 3.

4. The following will closely follow the central thematic in Koselleck's "Historia Magistra Vitae: The Dissolution of the Topos into the Perspective of a Modernized Historical Process" and "Space of Experience and Horizon of Expectation: Two Historical Categories," both of which are found in *Futures Past: On the Semantics of Historical Time*, trans. Keith Tribe (Cambridge, Mass.: MIT Press, 1985), 21–38 and 267–88, respectively. For other investigations into modern temporality see "The Future Cannot Begin" and "World Time and System Theory," in Niklas Luhmann's *The Differentiation of Society*, trans. Stephen Holmes and Charles Larmore (New York: Columbia University Press, 1982), 271–323, Giddens's *Modernity and Self-Identity*, and Peter Osborne's *The Politics of Time: Modernity and the Avant-Garde* (London: Verso Press, 1995).

5. Koselleck, *Futures Past*, 23.

6. Koselleck, *Futures Past*, 27.

7. See also Habermas's reading of Koselleck's thesis in "Modernity's Consciousness of Time and Its Need for Self-Reassurance," in *The Philosophical Discourse of Modernity*, 1–22.

8. Koselleck, *Futures Past*, 277. For a brief sketch of the historical development of the concept of horizon see Hans Robert Jauss's "Horizon Structure and Dialogicity," in *Question and Answer: Forms of Dialogic Understanding*, ed. and trans. Michael Hays (Minneapolis: University of Minnesota Press, 1989), 199–207.

9. For Koselleck, space of experience (the persistence of past experiences in the present) and horizon of expectation (the future made present, oriented to the not-yet) are to be considered formal categories. Neither what is experienced nor what is expected can be deduced from these categories; rather, they establish the conditions of possible histories. That is, history cannot be constructed or even conceived without the experiences and expectations of active human agents. As a result the "conditions of possibility of real history are, at the same time, conditions of its cognition. Hope and memory, or expressed more generally, expectation and experience . . . simultaneously constitute history and its cognition . . . by demonstrating and producing the inner relation between past and future earlier, today, or tomorrow." Koselleck, *Futures Past*, 270. While we need not pause to consider its apodictic certainty, there is much merit in Koselleck's position. For example, see Paul Ricoeur's qualified acceptance of Koselleck's claim in "Towards a Hermeneutics of Historical Consciousness," in *Time and Narrative*, trans. Kathleen Blamey and David Pellauer, (Chicago: University of Chicago Press, 1988), vol. 3, 214.

10. Koselleck, *Futures Past*, 257. Modernity, therefore, could be understood in the broad sense of the term as advanced by Luhmann: Modernity begins when traditional society, which is vertically differentiated into rigid strata, yields to a society horizontally differentiated into functional subsystems. See Luhmann, *The Differentiation of Society*, 229–54. If such a process began as early as the late Middle Ages, it was not until the late eighteenth century that functional differentiation began to consolidate itself as the dominant form of social organization. This is no doubt why Koselleck, in a parallel maneuver, retraces the emergence of modern temporality to a *Sattelzeit* —a "saddle time"—which roughly straddles, so to speak, the end of the eighteenth century and beginning of the nineteenth century.

11. We will have occasion to explore further past futurity in subsequent chapters which contrast it with its modern homologue.

12. Barbara Adam indeed reminds us that "to argue that ancient peoples led their lives in a 'perpetual present' or a cyclicality, where the past and especially the future have little bearing on their existence, denies those cultures something that forms an integral aspect of *all* life forms." However, there is a need to "distinguish between *being* one's past and future, having an awareness of it, and relating to this as an existential condition." *Time and Social Theory* (Cambridge, U.K.: Polity Press, 1990), 134.

13. M. M. Bakhtin, "Epic and Novel: Toward a Methodology for the Study of the Novel," in *The Dialogic Imagination*, trans. Caryl Emerson, ed. and trans. Michael Holquist (Austin: University of Texas Press, 1981), 13.

14. Bakhtin, *The Dialogic Imagination*, 16–17. The contrast with the modern novel is important here: "In ancient literature it is memory, and not knowledge, that serves as the source and power for the creative impulse. That is how it was, it is impossible to change it: the tradition of the past is sacred." However the modern novel "is determined by experience, knowledge and practice (the future). . . . When the novel becomes the dominant genre, epistemology becomes the dominant discipline." Bakhtin, *The Dialogic Imagination*, 15.

15. Bakhtin, *The Dialogic Imagination*, 15.

16. Bakhtin, "Forms of Time and of the Chronotope in the Novel: Notes Towards a Historical Poetics," in *The Dialogic Imagination*, 147–48.

17. Plato, *The Republic*, trans. G. M. A. Grube (Indianapolis: Hackett, 1974), 501b.

18. M. I. Finley writes that in antiquity, "the most radical critics either looked back to a more or less mythical past or they invoked a utopian vision . . . [yet] ancient utopias were regularly static, ascetic and hierarchical, not the sort of image that could arouse popular enthusiasm in the name of progress." "Revolution in Antiquity," in *Revolution in History*, ed. Roy Porter and Mikuláš Teich (Cambridge: Cambridge University Press, 1986), 55. See also Finley's "Utopianism Ancient and Modern," in *The Use and Abuse of History* (New York: Viking, 1975).

19. Plato, *Republic*, 546a. This is not surprising since Plato often portrays history as a cyclical process. In Plato's *Statesman*, trans. J. Skemp (London: Routledge and Kegan Paul, 1952), he invokes the myth of the golden age of Kronos, and writes of a divine power which guides the world to a certain apex, then releases it to allow a reversal of movement.

20. Aristotle, *The Politics*, trans. Carnes Lord, bk. 5, ch. 12 (Chicago: University of Chicago Press, 1984), Aristotle's critique requires him to equate Plato's theory of natural decay with historical decay.

21. Ronald Polansky, "Aristotle on Political Change," in *A Companion to Aristotle's Politics*, ed. David Keyt and Fred D. Miller Jr. (Oxford: Blackwell Publishers, 1991), 344.

22. Finley, *Revolution in History*, 50.

23. Aristotle, *Politics*, Bk. 2, ch. 5, 1264a1. My italics.

24. A. C. Bradley, "Aristotle's Conception of the State," in *A Companion to Aristotle's Politics*, 13. My italics.

25. *Zur Soziologie der modernen Forschung und ihrer Organisation in der deutschen Universität.* Cited in Herbert Schnädelbach's *Philosophy in Germany: 1831–1933*, trans. Eric Matthews (Cambridge: Cambridge University Press, 1984), 69.

26. Rudolf Bultmann, *History and Eschatology* (Edinburgh: Edinburgh University Press, 1957), 59.

27. St. Agustine, *The City of God*, ed. and trans. R. W. Dyson (Cambridge: Cambridge University Press, 1998), 412.

28. In his *City of God*, Augustine presents the history of the Heavenly City from Paradise to the Deluge (Bk. 15); from Noah to the Kings of Israel (Bk. 16); from the prophetic age to Christ (Bk. 17); and the history of both the Heavenly City and Earthly City from Abraham to the end of the world (Bk. 18).

29. R. A. Markus, "The Latin Fathers," in *The Cambridge History of Medieval Thought c.350–c.1450*, ed. J. H. Burns (Cambridge: Cambridge University Press, 1988), 105.

30. Augustine, Rudolf Bultmann suggests, "does not think of this struggle as a historical development moving with historical necessity to the goal of the victory of the *Civitas Dei*. He does not think of the *Civitas Dei* as a factor of world-history. . . ." *History and Eschatology*, 61.

31. Erich Auerbach, "Figura" in *Scenes from the Drama of European Literature* (Minneapolis: University of Minnesota Press, 1984), 72. For further elaboration on figural (*figuram implere*) interpretation see Auerbach's *Mimesis: The Representation of Reality in Western Literature*, trans. Willard R. Trask (Princeton, N.J.: Princeton University Press, 1953), 73–76, 156–62, and 555.

32. Augustine, *The City of God*, 903.

33. For more on these "revolutionary Christians" see Norman Cohn's classic study *The Pursuit of the Millennium: Revolutionary Millenarians and Mystical Anarchists of the Middle Ages* (London: Random House, 1970) and Malcolm Lambert's *Medieval Heresy: Popular Movements from the Gregorian Reform to the Reformation* (Oxford: Blackwell Publishers, 1992). For more recent examples of revolutionary interpretations of the Bible see René Coste, *Marxist Analysis and Christian Faith*, trans. Roger A. Couture, OMI, and John C. Cort (New York: Orbis Books, 1985), and John Marsden, *Marxian and Christian Utopianism: Toward a Socialist Political Theology* (New York: Monthly Review Press, 1991).

34. Augustine, *On Christian Teaching*, trans. R. P. H. Green (Oxford: Oxford University Press, 1997), 64.

35. See the introduction to *Medieval Political Theory: A Reader*, ed. Cary J. Nederman and Kate Langdon Forhan (New York: Routledge, 1993), 3–4.

36. A few major examples of such mirrors are John of Salisbury's *Policraticus* (especially Bks. 3–6), trans. Cary J. Nederman (Cambridge: Cambridge University Press, 1996); St. Thomas Aquinas's *On Kingship*, trans. G. B. Phelan (Toronto: Pontifical Institute of Medieval Studies, 1949); and Giles of Rome's *De Regime Principum*, ed. David Fowler, Charles F. Briggs, and Paul G. Remley (New York: Garland, 1997).

37. See his *Education of a Christian Prince*. For a brief assessment of its reliance on ancient political philosophy see pages 6–11 of James M. Estes's *"Officium Principis Christiani*: Erasmus and the Origins of the Protestant State Church" (*Archive for Reformation History*, 1992).

38. Machiavelli, *The Portable Machiavelli*, ed. and trans. Peter Bondanella and Mark Musa (New York: Penguin, 1979), 413.

39. Machiavelli, *The Prince*, trans. Harvey C. Mansfield (Chicago: University of Chicago Press, 1985), 22.

40. Eugene Weber, *A Modern History of Europe* (New York: Norton & Co., 1971), 185.

41. Hobbes divides science, "that is, Knowledge of consequences; which is called also Philosophy," into two subgroups: Natural Philosophy, which is knowledge of "consequences from the Accidents of Bodies Natural," and Civil Philosophy, which is knowledge of

"consequences from the Accidents of *Politique* Bodies." See his rather elaborate "table" in *Leviathan*, ed. C. B. Macpherson (New York: Penguin, 1968), 149.

42. Hobbes, *Elements of Philosophy: The First Section, Concerning Body*, ix. Quoted in Macpherson's introduction to *Leviathan*, 10.

43. The idea of creation is significant because establishing political society upon the requisite scientific foundations, which Hobbes claims to have uncovered, would resemble the authoritative act *"Let us make man*, pronounced by God in the Creation." Hobbes, *Leviathan*, 82.

44. It probably is no mere happenstance that the short-lived phenomena of *state of nature* theories, which began formally in early modern times, coincided with the increasing dissolution of premodern temporality. State of nature theories invariably ignore the experienced past and view the past somewhat abstractly—or better still, they look to a single pristine moment not yet touched by the vicissitudes of historical time. In certain respects, state of nature theories are the first modern utopian fantasies.

45. Hobbes, *Leviathan*, 150.

46. Hobbes, *Leviathan*, 130.

47. Hobbes, *Leviathan*, 161.

48. Hobbes, *Leviathan*, 169.

49. Koselleck, *Futures Past*, 278.

50. See Jürgen Habermas, *The Structural Transformation of the Public Sphere*, trans. Thomas Burger (Cambridge, Mass.: MIT Press, 1989), 14–26.

51. This study does not (and need not) subscribe to a single pattern of causation for the emergence of modernity; however, the transition from premodern to modern temporality could not but be helped along by the rise of capitalism. While not necessarily a causal relation, there is definitely a *correlation* between modern temporality and the rise of capitalism if only because the accumulation of capital required a future-oriented deferred gratification which, as Barbara Adam explains, "entails a certain trust, knowledge and expectancy of the future; in other words, the future has to attain a reality status." *Time and Social Theory*, 124. Moreover, J. B. Thompson reminds us that "as time was disciplined for the purposes of increasing commodity production, there was a certain trade off: sacrifices made in the present were exchanged for the promise of a better future." *The Media and Modernity* (Stanford, Calif.: Stanford University Press, 1995).

Chapter Two

Enlightened Future: Kant

Of Arms I Sing

Looking back on the intellectual activities of his century, Jean de Condorcet writes that the "philosophers of different nations who considered the interests of the whole of humanity without distinction of country, race or creed, formed a solid phalanx banded together against all forms of error, against all manifestations of tyranny."[1] Condorcet's use of the term *phalanx*, a highly successful infantry formation of the ancient Greeks, cannot help but conjure the image of war. One can easily imagine the philosophers of the Enlightenment arrayed in phalanxes, armed not with lances but with universal reason, marching off with the battle cries *Écrasez l'infâme* and *Sapere aude*, to combat all forms of error and all manifestations of tyranny. Of course, the image of a tightly organized and well-disciplined band of philosophers is not at all an accurate portrayal of eighteenth-century intellectual life. "In so far as they were united at all," writes a historian of the eighteenth-century intellectual climate, "it was merely by a generic or family likeness."[2] Still, the image of a battle has credibility, and while there were actually many battles fought, on numerous fronts and across a fairly long period of time, there was essentially only one war: the Enlightenment was a war against what was perceived as the tyrannical governance of the present by the past.[3]

Generally speaking, nearly everything that had been merely inherited from the past—knowledge, institutions, customs, traditions—was a potential enemy. Beliefs and doctrines, upon which rested existing knowledge, institutions, customs, and traditions, were put into question as the basic theoretical foundations upon which rested these beliefs and doctrines were increasingly being eroded by persistent economic and social change, and by an intellectual current that was increasingly and successfully replacing a worldview based upon the unintelligible and supernatural with a worldview based upon the intelligible and natural. If this could be said to be a war, then there can be no better example of the vanquishing of the enemy than when, on September 22, 1792, the Convention of Tuileries proclaimed a new Revolutionary Calendar—a calendar which began with the year I. Whatever else this calendar may symbolize, it can be seen as nothing less than an extreme manifestation of the Enlightenment ethos, representing, in effect, the severing of all ties with the past.[4]

The most immediate consequence of this war was the rejection of the past as an authoritative guide for the present and the future. Such a rejection in turn had a pronounced disrupting effect upon history and temporality. History always had been formulated with an eye to conserving a semblance of temporal continuity by relying on the authoritative nature of the past. Ancient and medieval chronicles and annals, for example, served to document the *flow of time*, but they rarely imputed ecumenical meaning to the mundane phenomena portrayed, while the *gesta* or hagiographies of this same period glorified the mundane by dispensing inspirational tales connecting the past to the present and providing edification and stimulus for future emulation.[5] A rendering of the past through the lenses of a codified tradition, along with the telling and retelling of celebrated myths and legends, effectively valorized the past, dwarfed the present, and overshadowed expectations of future excellence—change (even revolution, *re-volutio*) almost always meant a return to a former excellence. For centuries the past illuminated the present and the future, with the source of the light rarely being put into question. However, in an age when, as Diderot puts it, "all things must be examined, debated, investigated without exception," when all rigorous inquiry "must run roughshod over all these ancient puerilities [and] overturn the barriers that reason never erected,"[6] the source of light seemed an obvious target for scrutiny, which in turn, made it difficult if not impossible to preserve past certitudes, thereby disrupting the once stable temporal continuity that histories attempted to provide.

The modern shift in attitude toward the past in historiography is often attributed, and with good reason, to Pierre Bayle, the seventeenth-century historian, skeptic, fideist, and a relapsed heretic. Here lay the origin of modern critical history, an account and appraisal of the past which had an enormous impact in the following century. Bayle, in his *Dictionnaire historique et critique*, composed articles addressing an incredible number of subjects including persons, ideas, philosophy, religion, mythology, literature, and morality, and as Ernst Cassirer writes, it is through these articles that Bayle "freed history once and for all from the bonds of creed and placed it on an independent footing."[7] By critically evaluating historical phenomena, Bayle challenged what were for centuries the unchallengeable truths of the past—exposing the "hidden error which had survived through the centuries."[8] His *Dictionnaire* was an immediate success, it went through numerous editions, and it provided a brilliant foundation for the critical mind of the eighteenth century. It would not be incorrect to say that the enlighteners could trace their intellectual lineage to Bayle. With more faith in reason than Bayle, the enlighteners would continue his enormous undertaking. Like him, for example, as one historian writes, the enlighteners were not prepared to spare time-honoured myths, sagas and legends. Legends about the origins of monarchs and their peoples were called into question, especially that of the first Romans, Romulus and Remus, and their successors. Voltaire made fun of Joan of Arc and represented her as a superstitious peasant girl. Wilhelm Tell, venerated far beyond the borders of Switzerland, was unmasked as a 'Danish fairy-tale', since evidence of a 'shot at the apple' had been found in the Norwegian figure of Toko at a much earlier stage.[9]

Arguably the greatest casualty of this demand for historical accuracy was the traditional Christian view of the past. By the end of the eighteenth century not only was the Old Testament doubted as an accurate portrayal of the past, but the periodization based upon sacred history was also in Ernst Breisach's estimate "used less and less as markers in world histories by historians who increasingly preferred the theologically neutral scheme of ancient, medieval, and modern periods."[10] After Bayle, the past would be neither viewed nor understood the same way again, nor would it recover its once exalted status.

In addition to this increasingly critical attitude toward the past were the accompanying geologic discoveries that were providing evidence of an earth much older than had been previously believed. Geologic evidence of long-extinct volcanoes and fossils of long-extinct species and evidence of the rise and fall of the surface of the earth and the resulting sequence of strata suggested a magnitude of change over an immense period of time which simply could not be contained by biblical chronology.[11] It became evident that the earth had a long and complex *history*, as is reflected in the title of George-Louis Leclerc de Buffon's celebrated *Histoire naturelle*, a work which George Rudé reckons "exploded old myths and anticipated modern theories of the history of the earth."[12] The important point here is not that science had put into question yet another biblical truism, but instead that here emerged the idea of geologic time. It is easy to see how this idea could alter the way the past (and the future) is viewed. Releasing time from biblical chronology allowed the past to recede further from the present, thus allowing an expanse of time for complex and transformative changes to take place *in* the earth's composition and formation, while at the same time allowing for the imagination to extend time forward from the present into a distant future, providing time for complex and transformative changes *on* earth. The past extends backward, and, if only to give temporality a symmetrical balance, the future extends forward—granting enough time for enlightened projects, enough time to change human nature if needed, enough time, at any rate, to create a good future.

For the enlighteners this new attitude toward the past was for the best. While the past became at once more distant and less familiar, it also liberated the modern mind from the yoke of the past; it afforded a greater stature for the present and a greater confidence in the power to create a different and better future. It afforded, in other words, an opportunity to reinterpret and to reconnect the modes of time by reversing the valuation of the past and the future. This reversal did have its pre-enlightenment antecedents in the work of Francis Bacon for example, who anticipated modern theories of progress, and also in the work of Bernard Le Bovier de Fontenelle, who was perhaps the first to formulate a modern theory of progress.[13] Bacon argued that from the perspective of the chronological age of the world the ancients were not ancient at all. The ancients were actually the children of humanity and therefore not older and wiser. To think otherwise, says Bacon, is to have a mistaken temporal perspective because the "world's old age is its true antiquity and should apply to our own times, not to the world's youth, when the ancients lived. For their age, which from our point of view is ancient and older, from the world's point of view is new and younger." Bacon concludes from this that

> just as we expect a greater knowledge of human life and a more mature judgement from an old man than from a young one, because of his experience and the range of wealth of matters which he has seen and heard and thought about; so we can likewise fairly expect much greater things from our own times, if only they knew their strength and had the will to exert it, than from former times, seeing that the age of the world is now more advanced and enriched with a multitude of experiments and observations.[14]

Fontenelle concurs with Bacon, adding that the only real advantage the ancients had is that they came before us, and so they are rightly praised by their partisans as founders and inventors. However, since the ancients were really no different in mind or spirit than us, "if we had been in their place, we would have done the inventing; if they were in ours, they would be adding to what they found invented."[15] There is, he says, nothing mysterious about this, and coming after the ancients is actually to our advantage because we get to add to what they bequeathed. "Thus enlightened by the views of the ancients, and even by their faults, we not surprisingly *surpass* them. Only to equal them would require that our nature be very much inferior to theirs; it would almost require that we not be as human as they were."[16] Such a position is unacceptable for Fontenelle. Admonishing his contemporaries, he writes that "nothing so much arrests the progress of things, nothing so much limits minds as excessive admiration for the ancients."[17]

To be sure, the focus of Bacon and Fontenelle was less on moral, social, and political progress than on the progress of scientific and philosophic knowledge; however, such an irresistible idea could easily be employed in other spheres. With a new confidence in the increasing maturity of humanity, the idea of a progressive movement in history, of surpassing the past in both thoughts and deeds, took hold of the enlightened mind. By the mid-eighteenth century, writers such as Voltaire, Adam Ferguson, and Isaak Iselin were providing the first brief outlines of the idea of human progress, and they were the first of many.[18] And while, as Breisach points out, "no one work proclaimed and explained the concept of progress," and progress was instead "proposed, debated, and praised in many works," the belief in it "became sustained less by an agreed-upon theory than by a broadly shared *expectation*."[19] This expectation was reinforced through various theories of progress that provided not only a new temporal coherence for the modern world, replacing the idea of cycles or Christian salvation, but also promised, or provided the hope for, better things to come. One of the most succinct statements in defense of what was a guiding theoretical assumption of the Enlightenment, and, in various guises, of modernity, is found in Kant's *Idea for Universal History with a Cosmopolitan Purpose*—an essay that rivals even his *What Is Enlightenment?* both in its profound brevity and in the way in which it captures the optimism prevalent at the dawn of modernity.

Kant and the *Idea* of Progress

Kant's speculation on history provides a uniquely modern interpretation of the past and the future, and the way in which they are adjoined. Kant is aware of philosophical and political outlooks which contain or constrict future orientation. Central to Kant's critique of metaphysics and hence underlying his political philosophy is, as Frederick Beiser points out, the critique of hypostasis aimed at making "people self-conscious of their autonomy, their power and right to restructure their social and political world according to their will."[20] Such a theoretical position must counter that which reduces the future to a repetition of the past, whether it be prophetic histories or ethical-political theories. Indeed, Kant has little patience for the former, especially prophetic histories that view the human race as continually regressing (which he labels terroristic histories), or well-worn views propagated by cyclical histories (views which he considers farcical).[21] Kant has equally little patience for moral and political attitudes that confuse *is* with *ought*. Contempt is directed especially, but not exclusively, at political actors who purport that "one must take men as they are . . . and not as the world's uninformed pedants or good-natured dreamers fancy that they ought to be" without realizing that "as they are, ought to read 'as we have *made them* by unjust coercion.'"[22]

In his essay *Idea for a Universal History with a Cosmopolitan Purpose*, Kant offers a theory of history which valorizes not the past, but a future yet to be constructed. Kant understands the peculiar nature of a history being written from the vantage point of its future development; "it would seem," he writes, "that only a *novel* could result from such premises."[23] Peculiar yes, but typically modern. His aim is to posit an *idea* of a universal history, and this idea is "only a notion of what a philosophical mind, well acquainted with history, might be able to attempt from a different angle."[24] Progress, then, is only an *idea of reason*. The most important point to make about an idea of reason, without entering into the details of Kant's transcendental idealism, is that for Kant *reason* does not deal with things; it is rather *understanding* that deals with things. While the raw materials for understanding are the objects of intuition, the raw materials of reason are the "acts of understanding themselves" or the "employment of the understanding."[25] As long as the acts are not interpreted as things, then, Kant argues, reason has the clear responsibility to unite all the acts of understanding through pure concepts of reason, or ideas. Ideas play a role similar to that of the categories of the understanding: just as the understanding uses categories to unify, likewise reason uses ideas. Defined in a negative sense, ideas are merely judgments that have no corresponding object to be given in sense experience—they are simply heuristic entities.[26]

Here, the idea of nature offers a good example. Kant was diffident about the proper function of reason in the context of natural sciences. It was, to him, basically speculative, and the purpose of generating a regulative idea was a limitation on the function of reason that applied particularly in the realm of nature.[27] Its function is to introduce "unity into particular cognitions, and thereby to approximate the rule to the generality."[28] The idea of nature projects a sense of homogeneity in the world, which serves to suggest that the regularity of our experiences corresponds to something outside of ourselves—something more than a mere function of consciousness. In this sense the idea of nature, which is produced solely by reason, plays a vital though purely regulative role. As long as ideas of reason are not treated as possible objects of experience or as if the transcendental conditions of experience could apply to them, then ideas can play an active and a positive role in our conduct.

The idea of progress is just such an idea. As Kant puts it, if we first assume that nature does not operate without some kind of plan, then even if "we are too short-sighted, to perceive the hidden mechanisms of nature's scheme, this idea may yet serve as a guide to us in representing an otherwise planless *aggregate* of human actions as conforming, at least when considered as a whole, to a system."[29] Kant's idea would help to conserve temporal continuity by connecting the past with the present—not as an aggregate of timeless experiences but as a procession with a common direction toward a common end. Temporal continuity would be maintained but the past would be kept at a considerable distance from the present. From this perspective the past is essentially devalorized and becomes not a storehouse of exemplary wisdom to be plumbed, cataloged, and repeatedly applied to present circumstances, but instead becomes that which is continually and progressively superseded. The idea of progress is offered by Kant not to replace empirical histories of the past, but rather to present a clue to help decipher the history of civilization as a whole, a clue that alters the way in which the future is considered, which, in turn, effectively changes the way the past is viewed. That is, changing the outlook of the future consequently entails changing the way the past is considered. If unprecedented change can be expected in the future, then the immediate horizon must not be encroached upon by the past—the past must yield to the future or at the very least be neutralized.

Such a theory of history, of course, cannot duplicate the predictive character of mathematical sciences—which by the late eighteenth century came to be a standard for rigorous inquiry—where future events can be predicted from known laws of nature. In other words, as a regulative idea of reason beyond the legitimate realm of understanding, progress cannot be known to be a scientific, mathematically verifiable law of historical development; yet, since all phenomena, including human actions, are "determined in accordance with natural laws," finding a pattern or development within history, while difficult, cannot be considered impossible.[30] Where science fails or where reason reaches its limit, speculative philosophy—from a different angle—examines the past and attempts to demonstrate the possibility of an idea of progress in the development of civilization as a whole. By bringing a philosophical perspective to the history of the entire species, Kant undertakes to show that individual actions throughout history which on first glance appear alternatively as either confused or fortuitous, may instead display a definite, if somewhat slow, development of our original human capacities.[31] It makes no difference whether humans *consciously* pursued the development of their capacities because a philosophical meditation on the past allows for insight into a movement that was going on behind their backs, as it were, or even in spite of human actions to the contrary. From this vantage point, recognizing a pattern of development *in the past*, advanced through the unconscious and confused interplay of individual actions, does not, in and of itself, affirm subsequent development *in the future*. However, Kant believes that recognizing such development offers both "guidance in explaining the thoroughly confused interplay of human affairs *and in prophesying future political changes.*"[32]

This twofold shift in perspective is predicated on the bold assumption that nature works according to a plan. While contemporary political philosophy may consider this assumption as suspect, it was nevertheless a strategic and successful perspective for those enlighteners who wished to offer a coherence to the world without reference to the *super*natural. Kant is well aware of what follows without this perspective, especially since humans do not act purely on instinct as do other animals, and since humans have not acted according to some well-thought-out and consistently executed plan.[33] Without attributing to nature some kind of plan, Kant acknowledges that "no law-governed history is possible" and the "world drama" of individual actions would amount to no more than "folly and childish vanity" or "childish malice and destructiveness," while human history would amount to no more than an "aimless, random process" guided only by the "dismal reign of chance."[34] For Kant this counterperspective is depressingly unacceptable. Kant wishes to offer a different view, one that provides some speculative evidence for hope instead of despair.[35] Adopting his theory of history—if only as a regulative idea—allows the modern world to cast away fears and doubts about its future based on past experience, which until now has made us "despair of ever finding any completed rational aim behind it" and has reduced us to "hoping for it only in some other world."[36] With insight into the trajectory of history the modern world can replace various theories, which curtailed or limited our future prospects, with a theory which gives us the "*comforting prospect of a future* in which we are shown from afar how the human race eventually works its way upward to a situation in which all the germs implanted by nature can be developed fully, and in which man's destiny can be *fulfilled here on earth.*"[37] Kant's theory of history thereby advances a grand vision of the human condition in general, but more specifically the condition that humanity finds itself in the modern age. Experientially and theoretically at odds with the past, with no beaten paths toward the future, Kant aspires to convince humanity, as one scholar puts it, not of a "heaven beyond earth, but a goal for action, the just society on earth."[38]

Nature, Human Nature, and Times Past

Kant describes progress as the slow realization of a plan embedded and hidden in nature. This long-term plan is predicated on the axiom that "all the natural capacities of a creature are destined sooner or later to be developed completely and in conformity with their end."[39] Unfortunately, the time needed to execute nature's plan exceeds the life span of any one individual.[40] Since nature has seen fit to provide humans with a relatively short life span, progress requires a "long perhaps incalculable series of generations, each passing its enlightenment to the next, before the germs implanted by nature in our species can be developed to that degree which corresponds to nature's original intention."[41] Development therefore takes place over a long period of time; with a succession of generations advancing; with earlier generations laboring and preparing the way for later ones; with the past, in effect, paving the way for future advancement. Guided by nature, every generation stands on the back and on the foundation of a previous generation and only "later generations will in fact have the good fortune to inhabit the building on which a whole series of their forefathers (admittedly, without conscious intention) had worked without themselves being able to share in the happiness they were preparing."[42]

What is important here, aside from generational advancement, is that Kant admits that this good fortune is not, at least initially, attributable to conscious intentional activity. Before we can reach a level of being the self-conscious authors of our own future, nature must work *behind our backs.* Nature must bring us to the level where we can visualize and articulate a better future and *consciously* act upon it. Kant's theory of progress, therefore, can be divided into two distinct stages. Depending on the degree to which progress is extended through conscious intentional activity, the two stages thus can be labeled *predeliberative* or *deliberative.* In the predeliberative stage future orientation is limited and progress must work through seeds planted in human nature; and in the deliberative stage, progress is furthered by conscious, future-oriented activity.

The mechanism through which progress is extended in the *predeliberative* stage is conflict within society due to unsocial sociability. Kant defines unsocial sociability as a "tendency to come together in society, coupled, however, with a continual resistance which constantly threatens to break this society up."[43] Unsocial sociability thus can be seen as a combination of Aristotle's *zôon politikon* with Hobbes's egoistic individual: "man has an inclination to *live in society*, since he feels in this state more like a man, that is, he feels able to develop his natural capacities. But he also has a great tendency to *live as an individual*, to isolate himself, since he also encounters in himself the unsocial characteristic of wanting to direct everything in accordance with his own ideas."[44] The condition in society is one of antagonism, war and intermittent peace, where individuals compete for honor, power, and status, anticipating resistance and willing to offer resistence in the pursuit of such ends. This antagonism is not praised by Kant but it is not deplored by him either. As Kant sees it, antagonism "awakens all man's powers and induces him to overcome his tendency to laziness."[45] Without the unsocial aspect of human nature there would be no change, no culture, no development of human capacities, and ultimately no historical movement. The dual character of human nature is the way in which nature furthers its goal until we become conscious of the goal ourselves. Nature works this way because without the unsocial quality, which in and of itself is not admirable, human capacities would lie dormant and humans in general would live "as good-natured as the sheep they tended" and as a result "would scarcely render their existence more valuable than that of their animals."[46] Kant surmises that conflict precludes idleness and inactivity and promotes a condition of labor and hardships, which in turn fosters the need to actively seek out ways to lessen the labor and palliate the hardships. Through time, continual resistance and unsociability encourage and foster in man "new exertions of his powers and thus towards further development of his natural capacities" until finally,

> by a continued process of enlightenment, a beginning is made towards establishing a way of thinking which can with time transform the primitive natural capacity for moral discrimination into definite practical principles; and thus a *pathologically* enforced social union is transformed into a *moral* whole.[47]

Apparently, however, the conditions for the possibility of such a transformation emerge only in the modern age, and as a consequence all previous ages are thereby philosophically and hierarchically subordinate to this future social union.[48]

As Kant understands it, progress is not advanced through the collection of generational experiences accrued through cooperative social activity; advancement is made through social antagonism, which consequently imposes a circuitous—albeit unidirectional—progression through time. The past is constantly being outshone by this linear movement. Such a movement in history most certainly leaves an incalculable amount of debris and injustice in its wake with only later generations entering the building of human happiness built by countless, unhappy generations. This leaves little room for a nostalgic yearning for prior times. Kant's reworking of the past precludes its glorification, and is fashioned to eclipse theories which would have us wish for a return to a past *golden age*. Besides, as Kant writes in his *Conjectures on the Beginning of Human History*, this wish is really just an "empty yearning" reflected upon by poets, a yearning for a supposed bygone time where "we are content with the bare necessities of nature ... [where] there is complete equality and perpetual peace among men—in a word, where there is pure enjoyment of a carefree life, frittered away in idle dreams or childish play." While this is certainly a delightful vision, Kant shows little tolerance for it:

> It is yearnings such as these which make tales of Robinson Crusoe and voyages to the South Sea islands so attractive; but in a wider sense, they are symptoms of that weariness of civilised life which thinking people feel when they seek its value in *pleasure* alone, and when they resort to idleness as an antidote as soon as reason reminds them that they ought to give value to their life through their *actions*. The vacuity of this wish for a return to the past age of simplicity and innocence is adequately demonstrated by the foregoing account of man's original state. For as we have seen, man cannot remain in this state because it does not satisfy him, and he is even less inclined to go back to it once he has left it. Consequently, he must continue to ascribe his present condition and all its hardships to himself and his own choice.[49]

Simply put, Kant refuses to believe in a past golden age—an age which would warrant respect and maybe even emulation—and views all such *once upon a time* concoctions as hedonistic fantasies. From Kant's perspective such an orientation not only perpetuates undesirable fantasies but also proves to be socially and politically impractical. To be sure, before we become aware of a trajectory in history, we may indeed search the past for guidance, but once nature's *hidden plan* has been uncovered—which Kant believes he has done—we must guide our actions with an orientation toward the future.

Accordingly, the two stages established in Kant's theory of progress, predeliberative and deliberative, coincide with the epochal demarcation of premodern and modern. Once we become conscious of the trajectory of human history we enter the modern age, and we must orient ourselves toward the future. Kant's theory of progress, as outlined in the *Idea for a Universal History*, therefore can be seen as a theory of the movement from premodernity to modernity. Moreover, while in the predeliberative stage progress emerges from the gradual unfolding of an a priori plan hidden in nature and is thus teleological, its actualization does not preclude individual human effort and struggle. It demands it. Humans are neither governed by instinct nor guided by a predetermined plan nor endowed with innate knowledge. Nature has seen to it that any improvement of the human condition rests solely on human effort, even before we become conscious of this. In that nature seems to have taken pleasure in exercising the strictest economy and to have measured out the basic animal equipment so sparingly as to be just enough for the most pressing needs of the beginnings of existence. It seems as if nature had intended that man, once he had finally worked his way up from the uttermost barbarism to the highest degree of skill, to inner perfection in his manner of thought and hence (as far as possible on earth) to happiness, should be able to take for himself the entire credit for doing so and have only himself to thank for it.[50]

We are initially equipped with only the most basic instincts, and nature demands that we become the authors of our own future. From this perspective it appears that we always have had the power to create a better future but we were apparently never conscious of this power; we pursued many projects, but never a common project. But there is no predictable or guaranteed line of development, and ultimate responsibility for improvement is ours alone—to be praised if we succeed and to be condemned if we fail.[51]

Experience, Enlightenment, and the Unbounded Future

While the idea of progress, as with the idea of nature, cannot be an object of experience, at least the idea of nature has the advantage of being confirmed by experience, and "proves, and must necessarily prove, its reality in examples from experience."[52] While historical experience cannot muster the *same kind of proof* that empirical laws of nature can, Kant does think that there is at least some correlation between the idea of progress and historical experience. As he puts it, "the real test is whether experience can discover anything to indicate a purposeful natural process of this kind. In my opinion, it can discover *a little*."[53] This test is not applied to *past* experience, however. Kant makes it clear from the outset that he is only interested in supplying the guiding principle of a purposeful history, leaving it to someone more capable of writing an actual history in a manner suggested by his idea of progress.[54] Instead, Kant offers evidence of progress from *present* experience. Of course, it is not surprising that Kant believes that he can discover a correlation, however slight, between progress and historical experience by examining *present* experience; he lived during a most extraordinary period of Western European history, and he is often designated as the most representative philosopher of the age of Enlightenment. Moreover, his high opinion of the age in which he lived and its epochal significance is the foundation upon which his philosophy rests. As Kant sees it, one cannot help but experience the present as a time of unprecedented change and a transition to something altogether new.

In his well-known essay *What Is Enlightenment?* published just one month after his *Idea for a Universal History*, Kant expresses the epochal significance of the age as an evident departure from humanity's self-incurred immaturity: "If it is now asked whether we at present live in an *enlightened* age, the answer is: No, but we do live in an age of *enlightenment*," and there are present indications to instill a certain amount of confidence that "obstacles to universal enlightenment, to man's emergence from his self-incurred immaturity, are gradually becoming fewer."[55] Kant's definition of the Enlightenment is, as one commentator suggests, akin to the "passage from the status of a minor child to the status of an adult," hence, "enlightened modernity is the adulthood of the human race."[56] While one cannot fail to recognize the legal and psychological connotation of such a metaphor,[57] one also cannot fail to recognize its temporal connotation in the sense of a natural movement from one phase of life to another—indicating a singular linear direction from childhood to adulthood. Some of the present indications, or more specifically, some of the social, political, and economic *implications* of maturity that Kant enumerates in his *Idea for a Universal History* are the loosening of restrictions to private activities and worship, the general expansion of civil society and the market—where the pursuit of personal welfare adds to the vitality of business and therefore adds to the strength of the state—as well as the growing inability to infringe upon civil freedom without disrupting trade and commerce, thereby damaging the internal culture of a state and hence its external relations with other states.[58] These developments, among many others of this age of enlightenment, are forging the conditions for the possibility of mature social and political interaction, which in turn "encourages the hope that . . . a universal *cosmopolitan existence* will at last be realised as the matrix within which all original capacities of the human race may develop."[59]

Kant seriously believed (and few of his enlightened brethren would have seriously challenged his belief) that there was, at present, ample evidence to conclude that humanity was improving—and had indeed moved from a condition of barbarism to true culture—enough at least for Kant to view the changes taking place in the eighteenth century optimistically—as an age of enlightenment. Enough even for Kant to propose a theory of improvement enabling the ensuing radical and unprecedented changes to be placed in the context of a series of unique events developing in a common direction toward a better future, thereby making sense of a past that was increasingly receding, and connecting this reinterpreted past with current events taking place in his present. Progress, however, is more than a modern way of viewing the past; it is also a way of viewing the *history of the future*—of continuing advancement into an open future. For Kant, the time had come for the human species to take over the reins from nature and freely and consciously advance into a better future.[60] It may be said, then, that Kant's *idea* of progress serves as a sort of mental bridge from the past to the future; from predeliberative activity to deliberative future-oriented activity; from a history guided by natural necessity to a history constructed out of *free* conscious actions; from a premodern to a modern orientation toward the future. Hence, modern future orientation emerges when the *idea* of progress is coupled with the *idea* of free will. In a century intoxicated with the idea of freedom there can be no better example of its evident emancipatory potential.[61]

If humanity is indeed ready to take over from nature and work toward a better future, then it must be possible to freely impinge upon the present to construct this better future. Of course up to this point such freedom had never been attributed to humankind, at least not in this popular version. Such an attribution has always appeared to contradict fate, nature (laws of cause and effect), Divine Providence, or the like.[62] Indeed, the freedom to be conscious creators of the future, which makes Kant's theory of progress especially modern, would appear to contradict even the Kantian position that all experience—even human actions—are governed by natural laws. As Kant explains it in his *Contest of Faculties*,

> it is our misfortune . . . that we are unable to adopt an absolute point of view when trying to predict free actions. For this, exalted above all human wisdom, would be the point of view of *providence*, which extends even to *free* human actions. And although man may *see* the latter, he cannot *foresee* them with certainty (a distinction which does not exist in the eyes of the divinity); for while he needs to perceive a connection governed by natural laws before he can foresee anything, he must do without such hints or guidance when dealing with *free* actions in the future.[63]

Freedom is yet another *idea* of reason and, as such, it has the same disadvantage that the *idea* of progress has. But as an *idea* it also has the same practical advantage that other ideas of reason have, especially when viewed as a special kind of causal action. In general, if nature is the totality of conditions to everything that is conditioned, then freedom is the uncaused cause.[64] Being the uncaused cause, freedom cannot be part of experience, since experience is governed by natural necessity. Yet there must be, says Kant, "some experience or other which, as an event which has actually occurred, might suggest that man has the quality or power of being the *cause* and (since his actions are supposed to be those of a being endowed with freedom) the *author* of his own improvement."[65] Hence Kant is unsatisfied with mere speculative evidence of progress and wishes to present evidence from an actual historical event. The above passage is taken from a work written by Kant at the close of the eighteenth century—after the French Revolution—and the search for an event which exhibits this "quality or power" goes no further than the French Revolution. So, just as David Hume awoke Kant from his dogmatic slumber, likewise, the French Revolution, according to Kant, awoke humanity from its political slumber.

The French Revolution is at once both a "historical sign," which, when evaluating times past a posteriori, serves to highlight a tendency toward progress, and an event, which, through its epochal repercussion and its arousal of expectant emotions, remains causally active in the present.[66] The latter is particularly important because the immediate success or failure of the revolution itself does not concern Kant as much as its impact upon the "onlookers" of the political changes taking place.[67] What interests Kant is that the political changes taking place in

France, and elsewhere through the Napoleonic wars, have "aroused in the heart and desires of all spectators who are not themselves caught up in it a *sympathy* which borders almost on enthusiasm" even when the "very utterance of this sympathy was fraught with danger."[68] From this apparently universal reaction sweeping across Europe, Kant advances a no less sweeping interpretation: this reaction cannot "have been caused by anything other than a moral disposition within the human race."[69] Clearly, Kant believes that the arousal of expectant emotions unleashed by this unprecedented event has shattered the political limits of the possible based on past experience. In effect, the French Revolution represents a radical break with that which is past—that which denotes political immaturity. It also represents a forward march into a new future. In an extraordinary passage Kant contrasts the clash between the two opposing worldviews:

> No pecuniary rewards could inspire the opponents of the revolutionaries with that zeal and greatness of soul which the concept of right could alone produce in them, and even the old military aristocracy's concept of honour (which is analogous to enthusiasm) vanished before the arms of those who had fixed their gaze on the *rights* of the people to which they belonged, and who regarded themselves as its protectors. And then the external public of onlookers sympathised with their exaltation, without the slightest intention of actively participating in their affairs.[70]

This unparalleled solidarity is not *just* a historical sign of human improvement; it is for Kant improvement in and of itself. Moreover, and more important, it makes little difference whether the revolution is an immediate success, since this occurrence is so "momentous," so "intimately interwoven with the interests of humanity," that it will remain causally active in the present and simply resurface when more "favourable circumstances present themselves."[71]

The above shows to what extent Kant views the events taking place in his century as epoch-making. It is as if he recognizes that something completely new has occurred—an occurrence which has transformed the present into a time of transition and anticipation. As epoch-making, it is not a mere historical aberration to be easily reversed or simply brought back to its prior state. This is certain not only because the social and economic conditions for the possibility of a return to normalcy had been increasingly, and at times systematically, eliminated over the course of the century, but also because a temporal shift was taking place. The past had lost its essential meaning for the present, and an orientation toward the future could no longer rely on it for a sense of continuity and purpose. Fueled by a belief in the power to create a better future, radically new expectations had arisen—expectations which demanded fulfillment, and expectations which had no real parallel in the past: "for a phenomenon of this kind which has taken place in human history *can never be forgotten*," says Kant, "since it has revealed in human nature an aptitude and power for improvement of a kind which no politician could have thought up by *examining the course of events in the past*."[72] With this modern revelation, it is the future and not the past that must assign meaning, purpose, and continuity. And while Kant forecasts a continuing progressive improvement in the future, he cannot predict with any certainty the exact timing of the final result. He is willing to offer only a justification for hope—anything else would move beyond the limits of reason. However, there will be some unbelievers who may wish to dash even this justification for hope. Regardless, Kant asserts that his idea of progress is not just a pleasing idea to be recommended because of its possible practical effects; it is also a theoretically tenable idea. Furthermore, and more important, "if one considers not only the events which may happen within a particular nation, but also their repercussions upon all the nations of the earth which might gradually begin to participate in them, a view opens up into the *unbounded future.*"[73]

With this conclusion Kant gives a voice to the optimism of the Enlightenment. Philosophy, too, he says, has its *"chiliastic* expectations." Yet these expectations are of a different order than ones which simply await fulfillment. First, since these expectations are theoretically tenable, they are clearly not out of human reach; and second, not only can their fulfillment be realized by human effort, but it also can be hastened by conscious, future-oriented, political action. To be sure, Kant does put a somewhat conservative spin on such a radical idea. We must remain patient and not expect too much, too soon—if only to keep at bay those "politicians who would gladly treat man's hopes of progress as the fantasies of an overheated mind"—and we must accept that the direction of progressive change must proceed "from the top downwards."[74] Kant's idea of progress is designed to help prepare the way forward into the future; and, notwithstanding his conservatism with regard to political change, it is also a general call to action.[75] And even though the end result may not be reached until some remote time in the future, "it is especially hard," he says, "to be indifferent, for it appears that we might by our own rational projects accelerate the coming of this period which will be so welcome to our descendants."[76]

Notes

1. Jean-Antoine-Nicolas de Caritat, marquis de Condorcet, *Sketch for a Historical Picture of the Progress of the Human Mind*, trans. June Barraclough (Westport, Conn.: Hyperion Press, 1991), 141.

2. M. S. Anderson, *Europe in the Eighteenth Century: 1713–1783* (New York: Longman, 1987), 408.

3. According to Peter Gay, the *philosophes* generally agreed with John Locke's position that "at best an argument from what has been, to what should of right be, has no great force." Locke, *Two Treatises of Government*, ed. Peter Laslett (Cambridge: Cambridge University Press, 1963), para. 103. Cited in Gay's *The Enlightenment: An Interpretation*, vol. 2 (New York: W. W. Norton & Company, 1969), 92. In recapitulating a position put forth by Turgot, Anderson expresses the Enlightenment ethos similarly: "What had existed

proved nothing about what might, far less what should, exist in the future." *Europe in the Eighteenth Century*, 415.

4. It also should be noted that the calendar came to an untimely end in year XII (*anno Domini* 1805).

5. Ernst Breisach, *Historiography: Ancient, Medieval & Modern* (Chicago: University of Chicago Press, 1994), 98–106. Annalistic writings commonly used in the Christian world did portray a spiritual unity and hierarchically ordered cosmos but the meaning of secular phenomena remained esoteric. As Breisach writes, "God's decree governed all and it was for the most part mysterious. In such a world the records of events, besides telling of what happened, contained divine messages for human beings. An earthquake or a swarm of locusts warned people, a vision evoked hope, and the fate of an individual provided a lesson," 102.

6. Denis Diderot, "Encyclopedia," trans. Stephen Gendzier, in Peter Gay's *The Enlightenment: A Comprehensive Anthology* (New York: Simon & Schuster, 1973), 289.

7. Ernst Cassirer, *The Philosophy of the Enlightenment*, trans. Fritz C. A. Koelln and James P. Pettegrove (Princeton, N.J.: Princeton University Press, 1979), 208.

8. Cassirer, *The Philosophy of the Enlightenment*, 202.

9. Ulrich Im Hof, *The Enlightenment*, trans. William E. Yuill (Oxford: Blackwell, 1994), 262.

10. Breisach, *Historiography: Ancient, Medieval & Modern*, 199.

11. Norman Hampson, *The Enlightenment: An Evaluation of Its Assumptions, Attitudes and Values* (New York: Penguin, 1968), 91.

12. George Rudé, *Europe in the Eighteenth Century: Aristocracy and the Bourgeois Challenge* (Cambridge, Mass.: Harvard University Press, 1972), 153. The naturalist Buffon publically estimated the age of the earth at around 85,000 years, which made it considerably older than the biblical 6,000 years but considerably younger than the approximately 4 billion years estimated by modern geologists.

13. Of course, that progress is a *uniquely modern idea* has been attacked since the publication of Carl Becker's *Heavenly City of the Eighteenth-Century Philosophers* (New Haven, Conn.: Yale University Press, 1932), where he argues that the idea of progress has Judeo-Christian origins. Others have followed Becker's lead and have suggested, in a sort of infinite regress not uncommon in intellectual historiography, even earlier antecedents, such as is evident in the title of Ludwig Edelstein's book *The Idea of Progress in Classical Antiquity* (Baltimore: Johns Hopkins University Press, 1967). But probably the most famous and influential work in this vein is Karl Löwith's *Meaning in History* (Chicago: University of Chicago Press, 1970), where he argues that all modern philosophies of history (and especially progress) are mere secularized versions of Christian eschatology. It seems however that such works were written more to discredit the idea of progress than to show its ideational lineage. For a brief overview of this debate see W. Warren Wagar's "Modern Views of the Origins of the Idea of Progress," in *Journal of the History of Ideas* 28 (January–March 1967): 55–70. Moreover, for a brilliant attack on the secularization thesis of Löwith see Hans Blumenberg's *The Legitimacy of the Modern Age*, trans. Robert M. Wallace (Cambridge, Mass.: MIT Press, 1983).

14. Francis Bacon, *Novum Organum*, ed. and trans. Peter Urbach and John Gibson (Chicago: Open Court Publishing Company, 1994), 92–93. In less generous terms with regard to ancient wisdom, Bacon writes that "as to their usefulness, it should be said frankly that wisdom which we imbibed principally from the Greeks seems merely the boyhood of

knowledge, with the characteristics of boys, that it is good at chattering, but immature and unable to generate." "The Great Instauration: Preface," *Novum Organum*, 8.

15. Fontenelle, "Digression on the Ancients and the Moderns," in *The Idea of Progress since the Renaissance*, ed. and trans. W. Warren Wagar (New York: John Wiley & Sons, 1969), 52.

16. Fontenelle, *The Idea of Progress since the Renaissance*, 53. My italics.

17. Fontenelle, *The Idea of Progress since the Renaissance*, 55.

18. Im Hof, *The Enlightenment*, 7.

19. Breisach, *Historiography: Ancient, Medieval, & Modern*, 205. My italics.

20. Frederick Beiser, *Enlightenment, Revolution & Romanticism: The Genesis of Modern German Political Thought: 1790–1800* (Cambridge, Mass.: Harvard University Press, 1992), 32.

21. Immanuel Kant, "The Contest of Faculties," in *Kant: Political Writings*, ed. Hans Reiss, trans. H. B. Nisbet (Cambridge: Cambridge University Press, 1991), 178–79.

22. Kant, "The Contest of Faculties," 178. With regard to moral laws Kant's position is unequivocal: where "nature is concerned, experience supplies the rules and is the source of truth, in respect of the moral laws it is, alas, the mother of all illusion! Nothing is more reprehensible than to derive the laws prescribing what *ought to be done* from what *is done*, or to impose upon them the limits by which the latter is circumscribed." Kant, *Critique of Pure Reason*, trans. Norman Kemp Smith (London: MacMillan Press, 1993), 313.

23. Kant, "Idea for a Universal History," in *Kant: Political Writings*, 51–52.

24. Kant, "Idea for a Universal History," 53.

25. Kant, *Critique of Pure Reason*, 318.

26. Kant, *Critique of Pure Reason*, 318 and 550.

27. Kant, *Critique of Pure Reason*, 558 and 658.

28. Kant, *Critique of Pure Reason*, 553.

29. Kant, "Idea for a Universal History," 52.

30. Kant, "Idea for a Universal History," 41.

31. Kant, "Idea for a Universal History," 41.

32. Kant, "Idea for a Universal History," 52. My italics. Thus crucial for Kant is that, as Howard Williams rightly stresses, "conceiving of history in a teleological sense gives the added advantage of not only making sense of it for us, but also of opening up the possibility of realizing a purpose in the future development of man." *Kant's Political Philosophy* (Oxford: Basil Blackwell, 1983), 22.

33. Kant, "Idea for a Universal History," 41.

34. Kant, "Idea for a Universal History," 41–42.

35. *Hope* in Kant's essay is remarkable in its conspicuousness.

36. Kant, "Idea for a Universal History," 53.

37. Kant, "Idea for a Universal History," 52–53. My italics.

38. Beiser, *Enlightenment, Revolution & Romanticism*, 32.

39. Kant, "Idea for a Universal History," 42. The final outcome is less important for the task at hand than is Kant's general idea of human progress, but it is still of note that nature's fullest intentions can only be accomplished under a specific political constitution; the "highest task which nature has set for mankind must therefore be that of establishing a society in which *freedom under external laws* would be combined to the greatest possible extent with irresistible force, in other words of establishing a perfectly *just civil constitution*." "Idea for a Universal History," 45–46.

40. In his "Conjectures on the Beginning of Human History" (*Kant: Political Writings*, 232) Kant confesses that this shortness of life is the source of great dissatisfaction with the order of nature. On this he writes:

> It is true that anyone who continues to wish that life might last longer than it actually does must have little appreciation of its value, for to prolong it would merely add to the length of a drama made up of endless struggles with adversity. Nevertheless, we may excuse those of childish judgement who fear death but have no love of life, and who find it hard to complete each day of their existence with some degree of contentment yet can never have days enough in which to repeat this painful experience. But if we stop to think of all the care that afflicts us in our search for ways of passing a life as short as this, and of all the injustice that is done in the hope of a future enjoyment which will last for so short a time, it is reasonable to conclude that a life-expectancy of 800 years or more would not be to our advantage.

41. Kant, "Idea for a Universal History," 43.

42. Kant, "Idea for a Universal History," 44.

43. Kant, "Idea for a Universal History," 44.

44. Kant, "Idea for a Universal History," 44. Another, though less important, similarity with Hobbes (the "first" modern) is that like Hobbes, Kant views the past as one of war and struggles for peace.

45. Kant, "Idea for a Universal History," 44.

46. Kant, "Idea for a Universal History," 45.

47. Kant, "Idea for a Universal History," 44–45.

48. This does not mean that this union will come about any time soon; "it will happen only at a late stage and after many unsuccessful attempts." Kant, "Idea for a Universal History," 47. It is just that now moderns have the advantage of *consciously* and *deliberately* pursuing such an end.

49. Kant, *Kant: Political Writings*, 233.

50. Kant, "Idea for a Universal History," 43.

51. "This creation, unlike the mythical one of man, is conceived not as a singular divine act but as a continuing process in human history. It is the self-creation of mankind, understood as an infinite challenge." Hans Saner, *Kant's Political Thought: Its Origins and Development*, trans. E. B. Ashton (Chicago: University of Chicago Press, 1967), 14.

52. Kant, *Groundwork of the Metaphysic of Morals*, trans. H. J. Paton (New York: Harper Torchbooks, 1964), 123.

53. Kant, "Idea for a Universal History," 50.

54. Kant, "Idea for a Universal History," 42.

55. Kant, *Kant: Political Writings*, 58.

56. Garrett Green, "Modern Culture Comes of Age: Hamann versus Kant on the Root Metaphor of the Enlightenment," in *What Is Enlightenment? Eighteenth Century Answers and Twentieth Century Questions*, ed. James Schmidt (Berkeley: University of California Press, 1996), 291. Green's essay is important for his elucidation and critical analysis of the adjective *self-incurred* attached to *immaturity*. Green views Hamann's attack on Kant's use of *self-incurred* as foreshadowing twentieth-century criticisms of the Enlightenment.

57. According to Green, the legal context of the metaphor is often overlooked when the German concept *Unmündigkeit* is translated into *immaturity*; the "German term," Green writes, "emphasizes the legal rather than the psychological or behavioral nuances of immaturity." "Modern Culture Comes of Age," 292. Here we focus on the political implications rather than on legal or psychological ones.

58. Kant, "Idea for a Universal History," 50–51. With Kant's enthusiastic endorsement of such transformations taking place in the economic and political spheres in the eighteenth century, one can easily see why Kant is often not only considered the philosopher of the Enlightenment, but also the philosopher of the rising bourgeoisie. See Lucian Goldman's classic study, *Immanuel Kant*, trans. Robert Black (London: New Left Books, 1971).

59. Kant, "Idea for a Universal History," 51.

60. As Breisach reminds us, at the time this was a commonly held opinion: "The progress view had a firm support in the conviction of many eighteenth-century intellectuals that mankind had matured sufficiently to take its destiny into its own hands. God created the universe, set the orderly system of causes in motion, and from then it moved in Newtonian orderliness by itself. With the world rationally ordered and beneficent in essence, everything destructive in it was declared 'unnatural' and remediable." *Historiography: Ancient, Medieval & Modern*, 205.

61. Peter Gay writes that "the men of the Enlightenment united on a vastly ambitious program, a program of secularism, humanity, cosmopolitanism, and freedom, above all freedom in its many forms—freedom from arbitrary power, freedom of speech, freedom of trade, freedom to realize one's talents, freedom of aesthetic response, freedom, in a word, of moral man to make his own way in the world." *The Enlightenment: An Interpretation*, vol. 1 (New York: W. W. Norton & Company, 1966), 3. On freedom and political philosophy in the Enlightenment see Maurice Cranston's *Philosophers and Pamphleteers: Political Theorists of the Enlightenment* (Oxford: Oxford University Press, 1986).

62. As for the Christian belief in the inherent sinfulness of humans, which would preclude a belief in a general improvement, Kant has this to say in "Conjectures on the Beginning of Human History"(*Kant: Political Writings*, 233):

An account of human history will be of benefit to man and will serve to instruct and improve him if it contains the following lessons. It must show him that he should not blame providence for the evils which oppress him, and that he is not entitled to ascribe his own misdemeanours to an original crime committed by his earliest ancestors, by alleging, for example, that a disposition to commit similar offences has been passed down to their descendants; for there can be nothing inherited about arbitrary actions. It should show him instead that he has every justification for acknowledging the action of his first ancestors as his own, and that he should hold himself wholly responsible for all the evils which spring from the misuse of his reason; for he is quite capable of realising that, in the same circumstances, he would have behaved in exactly the same way, in that his first act in using reason would have been to misuse it (even if nature advised him otherwise).

63. Kant, *Kant: Political Writings*, 180–81.

64. Kant's philosophical position on freedom and natural necessity is complex and we need not pause to consider the details. Suffice it to say that while two types of causality are possible (one according to nature and one arising from freedom) one need not hold the disjunctive aspect of the proposition that *every* effect in the world must originate *either* from nature *or* from freedom. Kant puts forth an argument that allows for the possibility that an action can be considered *both* free and causally determined: "In thus regarding himself as intelligence man puts himself into another order of things, and into relation with determining causes of quite another sort, when he conceives himself as intelligence endowed with a will and consequently with causality, than he does when he perceives himself as a phenomenon in the sensible world (which he actually is as well) and subjects his causality to external determination in accordance with laws of nature." *Groundwork of the Metaphysic of Morals*, 125. The upshot of this line of argument is that there is no obstacle interfering with a free act—an act which also conforms to the mechanism of nature. That a free act does not contradict nature is one defense transcendental idealism can provide for freedom. Besides, it is not incumbent on speculative philosophy to provide us with full comprehension of freedom or how freedom is even possible. We do not comprehend freedom, only its incomprehensibility; but this is all that can be fairly asked of a "philosophy which presses forward in its principles to the very limit of human reason." Kant, *Groundwork of the Metaphysic of Morals*, 131.

65. Kant, "The Contest of Faculties," 181.

66. Kant, "The Contest of Faculties," 181.

67. Kant of course rejects the act of revolution or rebellion *tout court*. Here it must be stressed that he is concerned not with the revolutionary actors but with the spectators. However, that Kant can both reject revolution as a legitimate form of change while at the same time support the French Revolution is a difficult and well-known problem, and one which cannot be entertained here. For a brief analysis of this problem see Hans Reiss's "Postscript," in *Kant: Political Writings*, 261–63; see also Peter P. Nicholson, "Kant, Revolutions and History," in *Essays on Kant's Political Philosophy*, ed. Howard Williams (Cardiff: University of Wales Press, 1992), 249–68; and Beiser, *Enlightenment, Revolution & Romanticism*, 36–56.

68. Kant, "The Contest of Faculties," 182. Of course, as a professor in Königsberg, Kant was an employee of the Prussian state and knew of the danger firsthand.

69. Kant, "The Contest of Faculties," 182. This moral disposition is comprised of two convictions: first, the *right* of a people to live under a civil constitution of its own making, and second, that the only *right* and *moral* constitution is one that will by its very nature avoid wars of aggression (i.e., a republican one). Moreover, while Kant does not refer back to his earlier essay "Idea for a Universal History," it does not take much imagination to connect what Kant here observes as a kindling of a "moral disposition" with what he earlier refers to as the need to transform "moral discrimination into practical principles" (i.e., constitutional principles) in order to transform the "pathologically enforced social union" of the premodern age into a modern social union characterized as a "moral whole."

70. Kant, "The Contest of Faculties," 183.

71. Kant, "The Contest of Faculties," 185.

72. Kant, "The Contest of Faculties," 184. The second italics are mine. In his "Idea for a Universal History" Kant makes a similar observation with regard to the past, to wit, that changes taking place are preparing the "way for a great political body of the future, *without precedent in the past*" (51; my italics). Again, that what is taking place has *no parallel in*

the past is a central tenet of Kant's theory of history and his political philosophy.

73. Kant, "The Contest of Faculties," 185; my italics.

74. Kant, "The Contest of Faculties," 188. In a footnote Kant writes that *theoretically* devising political constitutions which conform to reason is one thing, but putting them into *practice* is quite another; it is the "*duty* of the head of state (not of the citizens) to do so."

75. Indeed, two years after "Idea for a Universal History" was published, Kant wrote that "each individual is for his own part called upon by nature itself to contribute towards this progress to the best of his ability." "Conjectures on the Beginning of Human History," 234.

76. Kant, "Idea for a Universal History," 50.

Chapter Three

Recapturing the Spirit of the Past: Hegel

Applying Thought to History

If the Revolutionary Calendar of 1792 can be said to symbolize the rejection of the past and the creation of a future ex nihilo, then the reinstatement of the old calendar in 1805 can be said to testify to the importance of the past, as well as to the shortsightedness of refashioning the future by decree. At least this is what Hegel would argue. A year after the new calendar became part of the past, Hegel was writing his *Phenomenology of Spirit*. While Hegel does not deny that the modern age is different from previous ages, he nevertheless takes issue with the idea of an unbounded future. In *Phenomenology* Hegel describes the modern age as "a birth-time and a period of transition to a new era" which is "dissolving bit by bit the structure of its previous world, whose tottering state is only hinted at by isolated symptoms." Furthermore, the unsettling of the established order and the "vague foreboding of something unknown" should be seen as nothing less than "heralds of approaching change."[1] A central feature of Hegel's philosophical enterprise is to interpret this approaching change. He does this by turning not to utopia, not to an unbounded future, but to the past—to history and the spirit of the past.

Hegel's theoretical position toward the past is articulated best in what appears to be a mere prefatory overview of historiographical methodology in his "First Draft Introduction" to the *Lectures on the Philosophy of World History*. Here he distinguishes three fundamental varieties of historical writings: original, reflective, and philosophical. The last emerges as the dialectical culmination of the previous two varieties. The details of the dialectical movement from original history through reflective history, culminating in philosophical history, are less the focus here than are the specific temporal characteristics that arise between the historian (subject) and events (objects) depicted.[2]

The distinguishing feature between original and reflective history is where *in time* the writer is situated with regard to the narrative, which, in turn, has consequences with regard to how the present is brought into the past or how the past is brought into the present. What Hegel denotes as original history is a history written from the perspective of those "who have themselves witnessed, experienced and *lived* through the deeds, events and situations they describe, who have themselves participated in these events and in the spirit which informed them."[3] Such a history is limited in scope—occupied as it is with individual acts, individual events, and circumscribed periods of time—and, due to an insufficient temporal separation between the writer and the events, this mode of historical writing is relatively unreflective. This is to say that, without mediation between the historian's consciousness and the object depicted, or because the "spirit of the writer and the spirit of the actions he relates are *one and the same*," adequate reflection upon the event is unlikely, if not highly improbable.[4] As a result, the depicted event's *specificity* in *historical time* remains unreflected upon, and hence the narrative fashioned out of what amounts to "subjective and fortuitous reminiscences," or "fleeting recollections," tends to detach events from the specificity of lived time and transport these past events "into a better and more exalted soil than the soil of transience in which it grew," thereby making that which was merely transient into something gloriously permanent "so that their heroes now perform for ever the deeds they performed but once while they lived."[5] However, historians such as Herodotus, Thucydides, and Xenophon, who exemplify this original mode of historical writing, are important because at the very least the lack of reflection counteracts the tendency toward projection: the depicted characters, in other words, express the culture and consciousness of their own lived time and not ones projected on them by the historian. For this reason alone, original history offers valuable insight into the spirit of a culture, of a state, or of a nation. Such histories can be read exclusively by those who wish to appreciate history—for those, to put it differently, whose aim is "not to become a learned historian."[6]

A more advanced mode of historical writing, from Hegel's perspective, is that of a reflective history. Reflection requires the writer to "cover *more than* just those events which were actually *present* to the writer" and to depict "not only what was present and alive in this or that age, but that which is *present in spirit*, so that its object is in fact the past *as a whole*."[7] So, unlike original history, which is less comprehensive and covers almost exclusively that which is most immediately present, reflective history requires *reflection* to abridge the multitude of events, or, what is the same, to *reflect* upon and explicate the essence or *spirit* of that which underlies the events. But more important, reflection is required to connect the past with the present, since, as Forbes explains, the "historian's consciousness and what he is describing have fallen apart," and the "past is now outside and different from the historian's consciousness"; thus the past and present occupy "separate spheres" requiring the past to be "consciously retrieved and made present in a way that doesn't happen in original history."[8] However, in an effort to transpose the past into the present what usually occurs is the opposite: the present is *transported* into the past. The error here, Hegel argues, is that "when the historian tries to depict the spirit of bygone times, it is usually his own spirit," his own cultural age, which "makes itself heard."[9]

So, reflective historians make a similar mistake as do original historians—neither have an adequate sense of historical time. Immediately connected to the events depicted, original historians tend to transport that which is past into an exalted, timeless realm; and lacking that which is an integral feature of original history, immediacy, reflective historians compensate by transporting the reader into the past, hence forging—or better still, forcing—an immediacy. Yet, forcing an immediacy ultimately fails because any attempt to transport the reader "completely *into the past* as something immediate and alive" can no more be achieved "than can the writer himself" be transported into the past, if only because the "writer is one of us, he is part of his own world with all its needs and interests."[10]

While attempting to make the past *come alive* by immersing the reader in the past is ultimately unsuccessful, it is also rather harmless when compared to trying to garner lessons from the past to be utilized in the present. The former errs by attempting to bring the *present completely into the past*, the latter errs by attempting to bring the *past completely into the present.*[11] Hegel agrees that gleaning illustrations of virtue from history is good for the soul and can be vital for *moral* instruction; however, such historical illustrations are certainly not useful for *political* instruction. This is because the "destinies of nations, the convulsions of states and their interests, predicaments, and involvements are of a different order from that of morality" which, therefore, make the "moral abstractions of historians . . . completely useless."[12] When Hegel writes that experience and history teach us that "nations and governments have never learned anything from history,"[13] he is not reproaching the shortsightedness or ignorance of nations and governments who are rightly advised of appropriate lessons of history but fail to utilize them. That reproach was often made in political philosophy texts prior to the modern age, but from Hegel's vantage point, such a reproach misses the mark completely. Hegel's point is much more extreme, and indeed, much more modern.

Reaching back into the past for models, right conduct, or the right course of action is ineffectual not only because "pale recollections are powerless . . . and impotent before the life and freedom of the present" but also because every political constellation is unique, and, therefore, "must make decisions with reference to itself alone."[14] This is a specifically modern teaching, a teaching that comes onto the scene when the gulf between the past and the present makes their reconnection theoretically problematic. A historical consciousness is required for learning this lesson, and it is only in the modern world that such a consciousness emerges. For Hegel, this lesson is equally applicable to historians, to political philosophers, and to political actors—especially the latter, since the pointless or, as Hegel would have it, insipid appeals to precedents set by Greece and Rome, which were made by some during the French Revolution, are perfect examples of regarding the distant past as somehow unsurpassable while simultaneously disregarding the actual, and to a certain extent unbridgeable, spiritual distance and difference between the ages.

According to Hegel, then, those who fail to recognize the distance and differing *spirits* between nations of different ages, whether they be historians, political philosophers, or political actors, or those who wish to make the past relevant by drawing up prescriptions from the past for application in the present, fail to recognize the corrosive power *and* the creative power of the passage of time—they fail to recognize, that is, the prerogative power of *historical* change. An account of this corrosive and creative power of the passage of time is what only a philosophical approach to history uncovers. Unlike original history, where the past and the present form an unmediated unity, where the past and the present are not properly separated and reflected upon, and like reflective history, where the past and the present require reconnecting, but unlike a reflective history which fails to give due consideration to the *pastness of the past*, philosophical history reconnects the past with the present by uncovering and making conscious the universal spirit of the past which inhabits the world as finite historical instances, uncovering that which is "eternally present to itself and for which there is no past" as it moves through time and creates or "directs the events of world history."[15] This *Weltgeist* is not an unchanging universal which transcends the historical world, but rather a universal that works its way to truth and actualization *in* the historical world.[16] Therefore, while a nation "can make its hour strike" but once,[17] and then wither away with the passage of time—taking with it the historical spirit of the nation (which is the universal spirit in particular form)—the universal spirit is conserved and transfigured (*aufgehoben*) into a *new* form, into a new nation.

To arrive at a proper understanding of this movement, its direction, and its ultimate aim, is the focus of Hegel's philosophy of history. Or as Hegel puts it, the "task of philosophical world history is to discover the continuity within this movement."[18] By discovering and making this continuity explicit, Hegel offers the modern world a way of connecting the past with the present, thus providing a temporal continuity that gives due consideration to the pastness of the past, but which also views the past as an integral component of the present. As a result, Hegel argues against those who wish to reproduce a path already beaten by the past, and against those who wish to simply devalorize the past and ignore it, or simply reject the past in the name of a completely different future—as if one could actually choose to reject one mode of time in favor of another, or accept the one over the other. Instead, Hegel integrates the past and the future into the present, thereby denying such choices.

Historical Change

Putting forth the somewhat distressing proposition that every age and every political constellation can make its hour strike but once, while simultaneously proposing that philosophy can uncover continuity among the impermanence of the past, which then can be employed to comprehend the modern present, is the central task that Hegel undertakes in his study of world history. Hegel acknowledges that the first fundamental category that presents itself when reflecting on the past is the category of change, and that this category generally proves disturbing. To be sure, it is hard not to recognize a "vast spectacle of events and actions, of infinitely varied constellations of nations, states, and individuals, in restless succession" which at first might strike us as nothing more than a "motley confusion."[19] Reflection leads to contemplation which in turn leads to "profound pity" and then "hopeless sorrow" for what has been witnessed: "It oppresses us," Hegel says, "to think that the richest forms and the finest manifestations of life must perish in history, and that we walk amidst the ruins of excellence."[20] Aside from the existential angst that is experienced from such a spectacle, the idea of change always has been anathema politically speaking. Stability is a primary objective of government, and for many centuries it has been a central motif for political philosophy.

Confronted with the notion of change, political philosophers invariably locate its cause in avarice, moral decay, sin, passion, and the like, and they expend substantial intellectual energy devising ways to curtail it, arrest it, eradicate it, or even ignore it. Indeed, the instability of change was the lot for a world ungoverned by philosophy, says Plato.[21] Aristotle, too, spends a weighty portion of his *Politics* (specifically Books IV–VI) outlining strategies for stabilizing various types of constitutions. Medieval political philosophy divides the world into a secular and a spiritual sphere, thus allowing for the theoretical acceptance of the transitory nature of the secular sphere, which requires princely force to ensure a modicum of stability, and thus allowing for true stability in a spiritual sphere—a world beyond this one. Hence, the idea of change invokes a confused, melancholic, resignation existentially, and summons a call to reaction politically. Both positions are but a response to the negative side of change—a lack of continuity and certainty and a lack of much needed stability. The concern for stability is a legitimate concern, Hegel confirms, and the idea of change in general is rightly considered a pernicious concept by governments. But for Hegel there is a positive side to change, and this he says is expressed in the following Oriental idea: "out of death, new life arises."[22]

This positive side to change, at least when expressed in the modern form of a "law governed process" and a progression "towards a better and more perfect condition," was a guiding ethos of the Enlightenment.[23] The Enlightenment raised the category of change from a vice to a virtue by placing change within the context of a generalized progressive improvement. In this regard the political thought of the Enlightenment makes an important advance. However, the enlighteners who advocated progressive change and the idea of perfectability made an elemental mistake, because change was raised to a political ideal by connecting it to the idea of perfectability, but the idea of perfectibility, in and of itself, has no content. Perfectability, Hegel argues, is "almost as indeterminate a concept as that of change in general; it is without aim or purpose, and the better and more perfect condition to which it supposedly tends is of a completely indefinite nature."[24]

Placing the value of change above that of stability, Hegel notices, is as widespread as it is attacked; and while it is predominantly attacked by those in government who are rightly concerned with political stability, it is also rightly attacked from a purely theoretical standpoint. As Hegel sees it, the idea of progress, as it is usually formulated with its underlying notion of an increasing change toward perfection, is unsatisfactory because "we are offered no criterion whereby change can be measured, nor any means of assessing how far the present state of affairs is in keeping with right and with the universal substance," and moreover, we are offered no "principle which can help us to exclude irrelevant factors," and finally, we are offered no "goal or definite end"; therefore, the "only definite property which remains is that of change in general."[25] In addition, when calculations are made, most doctrines measure sheer *quantity*, as a "constant growth of knowledge," or as an "increasing refinement of culture," or the like. In short, quantitative measurement begins with an object, say improvement, but is unable to discern any definitive conclusion from this object other than the comparative, more improvement. What is seriously lacking, according to Hegel, is the specific goal to be attained, which remains completely undefined. What is crucial for Hegel is that "we must know the goal which is supposed to be ultimately attained, because the activity of the spirit is such that its productions and changes must be presented and recognised as variations in quality."[26] What is needed is a theory which can discern qualitative progress rather than just quantitative progress. This requires that the process of change, which has been taking place in world history, is viewed not just as a form of progress, but as a form of historical *development*. In contrast to simple progress, the "principle of *development*," writes Hegel, "contains an inner determination, a *potentially* present condition which has still to be realised," and a potentiality "whose theatre, province, and sphere of realisation is the history of the world."[27]

This historical development of spirit is a form of progress and has certain similarities with natural development. But it is only insofar as change is common to both progress and natural development that Hegel's conception of historical change borrows from both these categories. His formulation of change is actually neither progress nor a natural development because, inter alia, neither have a place for the emergence of the totally *new*. Progressive change, Hegel argues, tends to treat the passage of time spatially, as it were, where mere *quantitative* extensions take place, which is different from treating the passage of time as a creative force where the qualitatively *new* emerges. And while natural change does follow a defined aim—in that an organism produces itself by making actual what it is potentially—and therefore makes a better model for change than mere progress, natural change is of a recurring cyclical kind which also does not allow for the emergence of something new.

With regard to change occurring in nature, Hegel writes that "the tree lives perennially, puts forth shoots, leaves, and blossoms, and produced fruit, and thus always starts again from the beginning," and while the tree can live for many decades, it too eventually dies. However, what is important is that the "reawakening of nature is merely the repetition of one and the same process; it is a tedious chronicle in which the same cycle recurs again and again. There is nothing new under the sun."[28] The development of spirit and that of nature, however, are not of the same order. The phrase "there is nothing new under the sun" is found throughout his study of world history, and Hegel's conception of historical change departs from the natural metaphor on this particular point. Change exhibited in the natural world, therefore, is not an entirely adequate model for change in the spiritual world because, while the view that there is nothing new under the sun is appropriate in the natural world, "it is not so with the sun of the spirit" because its "movement and progression do not repeat themselves, for the changing aspect of the spirit as it passes through endlessly varying forms is essentially progress."[29] This is a form of progress, of course, that exhibits the pattern of development that is found in nature—from potentiality to actuality, thereby providing a definite aim—while displaying a capacity for real change which includes the emergence of the *new*.[30]

Hegel likewise departs from the natural metaphor of development with regard to the actual process of growth: unlike natural development which takes place in an "unopposed and unhindered fashion," the sun of the spirit develops through conflict and struggle.[31] In the world of the spirit, Hegel explains, the

> process whereby its inner determination is translated into reality is mediated by consciousness and will. The latter are themselves immersed at first in their natural determination as such, which, since it is the spirit which animates it, is nevertheless endowed with infinite claims, power, richness. Thus, the spirit is divided against itself; it has to overcome itself as a truly hostile obstacle to the realisation of its end. That development which, in the natural world, is a peaceful process of growth—for it retains its identity and remains self-contained in its expression—is in the spiritual world at once a hard and unending conflict with itself. The will of the spirit is to fulfil its own concept; but at the same time, it obscures its own vision of the concept, and it is proud and full of satisfaction in this state of self-alienation. Development, therefore, is not just a harmless and peaceful process of growth like that of organic life, but a hard and obstinate struggle with itself.[32]

The mediation of consciousness and will and the struggle for self-knowledge are the *subjective* dimensions of spirit's self-realization and a counterpart to the *objective* dimension of spirit's self-realization in the theater of history.[33] An account of this hard and obstinate struggle is the primary theme in Hegel's *Phenomenology of Spirit*, and especially in the famous parable of Lordship and Bondage.[34] The parable offers a brief insight into interaction between the two dimensions in the process of development. For our purposes, the parable begins with a situation in which the knowing self takes what stands over and against itself as objectivity. In the process of trying to overcome this opposition of consciousness and objectivity, consciousness takes itself as an object of consciousness. To make itself an object in order to obtain knowledge of what it truly is, it must posit itself through activity. In the parable it is the labor of the bondsman which becomes the mark of freedom and self-realization. With the shaping, creating, and transforming of things, the bondsman imprints his own ideas on the empirical environment and comes to view himself, in the things of his creation, as a universal thinking subject and becomes who he is through the activity of his labor.[35] While consciousness requires the objectification of itself, which it accomplishes by creating objects through which it will then come to know itself, this self-knowledge and recognition are not immediate but rather follow successive stages of alienation. The essential progress of the critical reflection upon the relation of knowledge to its object is simultaneously the essential *progress* of the history of spirit. Spirit learns its relation to the world of *objectivity*, and what it is essentially, while at the same time becoming what it is through its empirical and finite productions—through, that is, morality, institutions, religions, and political structures. Since progress takes the "form of following the successive stages in the evolution of consciousness," then progressive development, which displays itself objectively in history, is "not just a quantitative process but a sequence of changing relationships towards the underlying essence."[36] Hegel's aim, therefore, is to uncover this development, and to uncover the transitions from one underlying essence to another which takes place *in* history—which is to say, *in* the underlying essence of the *state*, for historical change depends upon the state.

Historical Time

Hegel puts forward the statement that "among all the phenomena of history, our true object is the state."[37] For Hegel, placing the state at the center of his philosophy of history is not an arbitrary adoption of one object from among the vast array of historical phenomena. Instead, the state is adopted as the true object of philosophical history because the historical past only goes back as far as the emergence of the state; or to put it another way, history begins with the state. The word history (*Geschichte*), Hegel tells us, embodies two meanings: it denotes the "actual happenings, deeds and events" (*res gestae*) of the past, and the account or the "historical narrative" (*historia rerum gestarum*) of the past.[38] The combination of both the subjective and objective meanings of history, Hegel claims, "should be recognized as belonging to a higher order than that of mere external contingency"; therefore, "we must in fact suppose that the writing of history and the actual deeds and events of history make their appearance simultaneously, and they emerge together from a common source."[39] As Hegel sees it, this common source is the state because "it is the state which first supplies a content which not only lends itself to the prose of history but actually helps to produce it."[40] The state replaces subjective "dictates of authority" with objective "formal commands and laws" or "general and universally valid directives," and in doing so the state "creates a record of its own development," thereby creating an objective, written, past—a memory of itself or an objective reference point in history—from which a subjective historical narrative can be fashioned.[41]

Hegel insists that the appearance of the state is a condition for the possibility of history itself. Yet, when Hegel claims that history begins with the state, whatever else this claim may entail, it does not entail that there is no past before the emergence of the state. What Hegel does seem to claim, however, is that because there is no written record of universal significance before the emergence of the state, there is no *historical past* before the emergence of the state. The past that predates the state is, for Hegel, a *pre*historical period, a period that may have indeed produced other records of *its past* in lieu of written records (archeological records, for example), but such records lie outside the confines of Hegel's investigation.[42] Thus, Hegel spends little effort speculating on the past before written history, and he eschews fabricating a *state of nature* which had been a favorite way of considering the past for many modern political philosophers before Hegel. Instead, Hegel considers the prehistorical period a *voiceless past*, which is not really suitable for philosophical exploration. Enquiry must begin alternatively "at that point where rationality begins to manifest itself in worldly existence"; it is only at this point that history becomes an object befitting serious philosophical study.[43] A philosophical history, Hegel argues, requires an object that conjoins the two meanings of history—subjective and objective meanings—and the prehistorical period or periods which

> elapsed in the life of nations before history came to be written, and which may well have been filled with revolutions, migrations, and the most violent changes, have no objective history precisely because they have no subjective history, i.e. no historical narratives. It is not that the records of such periods have simply perished by chance; on the contrary, the reason why we have no records of them is that no such records were possible. It is only within a state which is conscious of its laws that clearly defined actions can take place, accompanied by that clear awareness of them which makes it possible and necessary to commit them to posterity.[44]

In the period before the state, therefore, events such as revolutions, or migrations, or violent changes have yet to attain the status of history—the status of world-historical events—from which philosophy can discern a meaning and delineate the contours of its development.[45]

Moreover, the prehistorical period may well have exhibited change, but not developmental change. Developmental change becomes possible only with the appearance of the state. Hegel uses the Greek myth of Kronos and Zeus to illustrate this crucial distinction between what can be described as a sort of changeless change in the prehistorical period, and a developmental change in the historical period. As Hegel sees it "if nations are impelled by desires, their deeds are lost without a trace (as with all fanaticism), and no enduring achievement remains. Or the only traces they leave are ruin and destruction."[46] Such a condition, Hegel writes, is characteristic of an age which the ancient Greeks had proclaimed as the Golden Age of Kronos, the god of Time.[47] The rule of Kronos, "who devoured his children (i.e. the deeds he has himself produced)," was an age which "produced no ethical works," no lasting accomplishments.[48] But when Zeus dethroned his father, Kronos, he delivered forth reason (Pallas Athena) and the arts (the Muses), and he was "able to check the power of time" by creating a "conscious ethical institution, i.e. by producing the state."[49] This *rational* and *creative* act of the "political god" Zeus, which established a political organization resting upon rational and moral foundations, arrested the purely negative or corrosive power of time by instituting something that endures in and through time. Whatever else Hegel may have had in mind with his brief recounting of the ancient myth, it is clear that to *arrest* time is significantly different than to *conquer* time, and the truth of the myth is not that time comes to an end with the rational and creative act of Zeus, but rather that *historical time* begins with it.

The state is a product of thought, so while thought can arrest the power of time it can do so only by placing itself, or particularizing itself into time. Thus, time is able to exact a revenge of sorts by eroding the *particular* rational and moral foundations upon which the state rests. However, the result of this revenge is not changeless change but progressive, developmental change. This is because the *agent of change* is now the universalizing dynamic of thought itself—the selfsame rational thought which gave the state its content, and which gave rise to history in the first place. Hegel sees this change as following a distinct pattern—a historical dialectic, as it were. He writes that the "highest point in the development of the nation is reached when it has understood its life and condition by means of thought, and acquired a systematic knowledge of its laws, justice, and ethical life; for in this achievement lies the closest possible unity which the spirit can attain with itself."[50] This self-conscious reflection and representation of the laws, justice, and ethical life of a nation are consequently "different in form from the real activity, the real work and life which made such an achievement possible," and as a result, the "nation now has both a real and an ideal existence."[51] Ever searching for the essence behind appearance, thought liberates itself from the determinate content of external restraints, thus becoming "conscious to some degree of limitation of such determinate things as belief, trust, and custom, so that the consciousness now has reasons for renouncing the latter and the laws which they impose."[52] A contradiction or an opposition thus emerges between this real and ideal existence that can only be resolved, Hegel argues, in favor of thought—towards the *newly* developed universal principle which, in turn, compels both the dissolution of the existing social and political life, and the production of a social and political life that embody this *new* universal principle. "And thus Zeus," Hegel conveys in a beautiful passage, "who set limits to the depredations of time and suspended its constant flux, had no sooner established something inherently enduring than he was himself devoured along with his whole empire. He was devoured by the principle of thought itself, the progenitor of knowledge, of reasoning, of insight based on rational grounds, and of the search for such grounds."[53]

True, but out of this death, a new life emerges. The corrosive activity of thought, as Hegel puts it, is the "source and matrix from which a new form—and indeed a *higher form*, whose principle both conserves and transfigures it—emerges."[54] Of course, this may neither succor the nation which has made *its hour strike*, and which now can only become part of the historical past, nor provide support for those who view the dissolution of the old life as being somehow reversible, but such is the movement, the process, and the *progress* of world history. Furthermore, the change that occurs with the dissolution of one political constellation and the birth of another is not an arbitrary substitution of one principle for another, which would make continuity among changes impossible, and it is not a mere periodic modification of regimes because of, say, inept rulers, or the disobedience of the ruled, or some sort of natural political entropy, or the like, which could be explained in terms of Platonic periodic cycles.[55] On the contrary, since each new principle or form is the transfigured product of that which preceded it, and since this transfiguration is from a lesser to a higher form, historical change can be viewed as a chain of successive stages with a specific direction toward a definite aim. Individually, each stage is but a "link in the chain of the world spirit's development,"[56] a link in a chain that stretches across time from the beginning of the historical past to the present. And since each stage can only be viewed as a historically specific epoch, one lesson becomes obvious, and this is that political

constitutions under which the world-historical nations have blossomed are peculiar to them, and should not therefore be seen as universally applicable. Their differences do not simply consist in the particular way in which they have elaborated and developed a common basis, but in the distinct nature of the principles which underlie them. No lessons can therefore be drawn from history for the framing of constitutions in the present. For the latest constitutional principle, the principle of our times, is not to be found in the constitutions of the world-historical nations of the past.[57]

Clearly, this is not a radical and systematic denial of the past, but a radical and systematic denial that the political world can move against the flow of *historical time* and resuscitate social and political constellations of the past—something that from Hegel's perspective is not just politically undesirable but logically impossible. To be sure, Hegel concedes that one may indeed find a "Greek nation with its noble paganism" or a "Roman one of the same kind" existing somewhere in the present, but make no mistake about it, these nations "belong to the past."[58] Each nation embodies but one universal principle, which is incorporated into the constitutional structure of the state, and but one aim, which, once attained, has no additional role to play and is forced to yield its leading role in the theater of world history. All states pass through stages of growth, decay, and dissolution. The dissolution of an old political constellation gives rise to a new (more developed) political constellation, a new nation with new constitutional principles that are incorporated into the state. Embedded within time, old political constellations become part of the historical past, existing not only in historical memory, but also as links in the temporal chain of the development of *Weltgeist*; links which, once uncovered and connected together by a philosopher (in this case Hegel) who glances backward from the present, provide coherence and continuity to a past that had become more distant and less familiar, and a past that had become increasingly viewed as a "motley confusion" of superstition, of error, and of irrationality. Moreover, besides providing coherence and continuity, this backward glance uncovers a *definite* and *rational* development toward a definite and rational aim—the "history of the world accordingly represents the successive *stages* in the development of that principle whose substantial content is the consciousness of freedom."[59]

As Hegel sees it, to view history philosophically is to view it in light of this ultimate aim of history.[60] A philosophy of history must therefore consider the particular manifestations of the development of freedom and therefore must consider the development of human freedom as it develops in the "theatre of world history."[61] Again, the main character on this stage of world history is the state. It is the state to which, as Hegel says, "individuals react from birth with trust and habit, in which they have their being and reality, their knowledge and volition, and through which they acquire and preserve their worth." The basic plot centers around the dialectical conflict (opposition and negation) between the "substantial freedom" of the state and the "realm of subjective freedom" of the individual.[62] The dialectical conflict between these two determinations of freedom generate and advance the progress of history toward an ultimate reconciliation between them.[63] This progress has both spacial (geographical) and temporal (historical) dimensions; it follows a course from east to west and it consists of four historical phases: the Oriental World, where subjective freedom is undeveloped, and which is characterized by Hegel as the childhood of humanity; the Greek World, where subjective freedom has its origin, and which is likened to the adolescence of humanity; the Roman World, where individual actions are subsumed within the state, and which is considered by Hegel as the manhood of history; and finally, the Germanic

World, which covers the birth of Christianity, the Middle Ages, and the modern world, and which is likened to the old age of humanity.[64]

The Apotheosis of History: The Modern Present

While the course of historical development of freedom moves geographically from east to west, and while it moves temporally through six thousand years, Hegel considers it (philosophically speaking) as but a day's work.[65] This *day* is the present; indeed from Hegel's standpoint, it is the *modern present*, the old age of humanity, where the luminous essence of the past is grasped.[66] As Hegel explains, in "our understanding of world history, we are concerned with history primarily as a record of the past. But we are just as fully concerned with the present," which, contains "all the stages which appear to have occurred earlier in history."[67] Hegel wishes to comprehend the modern present by recapturing the spirit of the past. He was not the only German to stress the importance of the past in that the "most distinctive contribution of the Germans to the intellectual history of this period was their sense of history itself, so glaringly absent in the French and English ideologies."[68] But Hegel's philosophy of history is really a *philosophy of the present*—his present, and the transfigured past within his present. The present, in other words, is what Hegel wishes to understand when he looks into the past; and in 1806 Hegel ended one of his lectures by underscoring the fact that it is precisely his present that needed to be understood because he and his contemporaries find themselves

> in an important epoch, in a fermentation, in which Spirit has made a leap forward, has gone beyond its previous concrete form and acquired a new one. The whole mass of ideas and concepts that have been current until now, the very bonds of the world, are dissolved and collapsing into themselves like a vision in a dream. A new emergence of spirit is at hand; philosophy must be the first to hail its appearance and recognize it, while others resisting impotently, adhere to the past, and the majority unconsciously constitute the matter in which it makes its appearance.[69]

This passage expresses three important facets of Hegel's political philosophy. First, Hegel is unwavering in his belief that he is living in a distinctly new epoch in the history of humanity. This is enthusiastically declared in his *Phenomenology of Spirit*, where he uses the metaphor of a birth-time to describe the new age in which he lives, and it is clearly expressed in his later, more mature works.[70] In fact it would not be an overstatement to claim that this belief *is* what undergirds his entire philosophy. Second, when Hegel asks a question such as "Who has stood among the ruins of Carthage, Palmyra, Persepolis or Rome without being moved to reflect on the transience of empires and men, to mourn the loss of the rich and vigorous life of bygone ages?"[71] he is addressing his contemporaries—or at least those contemporaries who *impotently* cling to that which has *passed*. Again, Hegel understands that the transient quality of history is distressing, and especially so for those who are witnessing the collapse of old bonds firsthand. However, that which has passed is unretrievable. This is the lesson Hegel wishes to teach the modern world; but it is also a lesson that had become increasingly evident because, as Manfred Riedel reminds us, "one of the characteristic marks of the waning eighteenth century was that, as a result of the fact that it took up the political concepts of the ancients, it became aware of its distance from antiquity, from the old civic freedom of the Greeks and Romans." And thus "for the first time in the history of the European political tradition this assimilation lacked 'application' to the historical realities of the time."[72] Third, instead of lamenting the past Hegel gives philosophical expression to what he considered to be the *last act* of a long and painful human drama. Europe was in the midst of giving birth to a new world and, more specifically, a new ethical life. Through his philosophy Hegel wishes to mark and acknowledge the appearance of this new world and its attendant ethical life. It is here that Hegel's philosophy of history meets his political philosophy of the modern state as expounded in the *Philosophy of Right*.

What Hegel wants the modern world to recognize is that the modern state is the product of a long journey through *historical time*, and therefore past forms of the state are *sublated* in its present form. In principle, the modern state embodies a fully developed ethical life. The "essence of the state is ethical life," and ethical life (*Sittlichkeit*) "consists in the unity of the universal and subjective will,"[73] and this unity is, as Hegel states in the *Philosophy of Right*, "freedom realized, the absolute end and aim of the world."[74] At the center of Hegel's conception of ethical life is the community. A truly moral and meaningful life requires a community where one can participate as a member. Or more precisely, the good life cannot be attained individually; it can be attained only through the participation in a larger community.[75] This all-embracing image of community, where an individual attains a sense of belonging, has as its contrast an image of life—indeed what modern life seems to have become—in which the individual and the community are firmly distinguished, or in which individual interests and the interests of others are considered perpetually antagonistic. Hegel's conception of ethical life has as its image a community life characteristic of the ancient Greeks, where individual interests and community interests were harmonious. Ancient Greek life, as Hegel understood it, was a collective life that gave its members a common experience and a higher meaning, where ethical ideals permeated social life, and where the interests of the community and the interests of the individual were ideally identical. It is hard not to notice the admiration that Hegel has for this ancient form of social life. "His writing about ancient *Sittlichkeit*," writes one commentator, "reveals a feeling of loss, even a yearning for a return to this simpler and more harmonious way of relating to the social world."[76] However, Hegel does not suggest that the modern world should attempt to recover this simpler form of life—even if it were possible, which, according to his philosophy of history, it is not. That this life was more simple, primitive, and underdeveloped, is the problem. Hegel's philosophy reveals that the community life of the ancients was an imperfect embodiment of ethical life because the essential moment of particularity (individuality or subjective freedom) was undeveloped.

A fully developed ethical life demands the mutual reconciliation of subjective particularity with the objective order: subjectively, the right of individuals to their particular satisfaction must be contained in the fully developed ethical order, while objectively, the right of individuals to be subjectively destined to freedom is fulfilled only when they belong to an actual ethical order.[77] The emergence of subjective particularity in the ancient world, which for Hegel dates from the time of Socrates, is the "moment which appeared in the ancient world as an invasion of ethical corruption and the ultimate cause in that world's downfall."[78] The ethical life of the ancient Greeks was corrupted by the development of subjective particularity because the ancient state could not reconcile it with the good of the whole. And this apparent irreconcilability, according to Hegel, is reflected in the political theory of Plato, as he could only cope with subjective particularity by denying its right and excluding it from his ideal state. Such is always the consequence when the life of a nation brings forth new fruit; this new fruit cannot "fall back into the womb from which it emerged; the nation itself is not permitted to enjoy it, but must taste it instead in the form of a bitter draught."[79]

This fruit, after subsequent ripening over the course of history, is enjoyed only in the modern world. As Hegel sees it, the "right of the subject's particularity or the right of subjective freedom is the pivot and center of the difference between antiquity and modern times."[80] The right of subjective freedom is achieved only with the emergence and expansion of civil society (*bürgerliche Gesellschaft*). Civil society is a form of association that coincides with the growth, expansion, and consolidation of a *modern* market economy, and with the rise of the bourgeoisie, and had become a much thematized subject of seventeenth- and eighteenth-century political philosophy.[81] It is generally agreed that Hegel is the "representative theorist of civil society," largely because, as Jean Cohen and Andrew Arato write, "he was the first and most successful in unfolding the concept as a theory of a highly differentiated and complex social order."[82] Moreover, Hegel is rightly credited with being the first to conceptually differentiate civil society from political society (or the state), which is now commonplace, but which had remained conceptually undifferentiated from Aristotle to Kant.[83] According to Hegel, civil society is an essential component for ethical life because it is where particularity gets its due, it is where the "right of individuals to their particular satisfaction" manifests itself.[84] This right is what was lacking in the ethical life of the ancients. Subsequent historical development was needed for its addition into ethical life, and it had to wait until the creation of civil society, which is the grand "achievement of the modern world which for the first time gives all determinations of the Idea their due."[85] Civil society is that *newly* developed social sphere characteristic of the modern market economy where individuals (as private persons) pursue their own particular interests to satisfy their own particular needs. Civil society is animated by two interconnected principles, according to Hegel. The first is the pursuit of particular needs by individuals who behave with a "mixture of caprice and physical necessity." The second principle stems from the fact that each particular person can only satisfy particular needs by interacting with other persons who are also seeking the private satisfaction of needs; therefore, a "particular person is essentially so related to other particular persons that each establishes himself and finds satisfaction by means of the others."[86] These two principles form what Hegel describes as a "system of complete interdependence, wherein the livelihood, happiness, and legal status of one man is interwoven with the livelihood, happiness, and rights of all."[87] Hence, a system of mutual dependence is obtained whereby individual interests are pursued which, in turn, promote the interest of the whole. Hegel maintains, therefore, that particularity is conditioned by universality, in that by interacting with the property, the product, and the needs of others, the universal "asserts itself in the bearing which this satisfaction has on the needs of others and their free arbitrary wills."[88]

From this brief account of civil society as understood by Hegel, it is easy to concur with the observation that "Hegel's understanding of civil society was strongly influenced by his intimate knowledge of the classical theorists of political economy: Ricardo, Say, Smith, and Steuart."[89] What is uniquely Hegelian, however, is the stress he places upon the disruptive power of subjective particularity that must be "held in check by the power of universality," not the least because "civil society affords a spectacle of extravagance and want as well as of the physical and ethical degeneration common to both."[90] And while it is true, as Shlomo Avineri points out, that "Hegel integrates the Smithian model of a free market into his philosophical system, by transforming Smith's 'hidden hand' into dialectical reason working in civil society,"[91] it is equally true that this hidden hand, by itself, cannot ensure the common good. For Hegel, true reconciliation with the common good is not the task of *civil society* but instead the task of the modern *state*.

The principle of the modern state, properly understood, reconciles subjective freedom (which corrupted and destroyed the ancient community) with the universal ends of the community.[92] The principle of the modern state, in Hegel's view, can produce this reconciliation not only because philosophy reveals that the unity is possible and essential to ethical life, and not only because the essential moments for this reconciliation are present, but also because the principle of the modern state has prodigious strength which allows "subjectivity to progress to its culmination in the extreme of self-subsistent personal particularity, and yet at the same time brings it back to the substantive unity and so maintains this unity in the principle of subjectivity itself."[93] As Hegel sees it, modern freedom requires the recognition and complete development of particular interests, and it is the principle of the modern state to allow the extreme development of particularity and yet *brings it back* in order to reconcile it with the universal, thereby achieving substantive unity or the good of the community. As a community, the modern state is not composed of individuals (nor even the aggregate interests of individuals); rather, individuals are mediated through a series of associations, institutions, and corporations before *reaching* citizenship in the state. The political institutions of the modern state (a hereditary monarchy, which serves as a symbol of the unity of the modern state; a state bureaucracy, which serves the universal interests of the state; and an assembly of estates, where representation is based on membership in either the monarchy, the bureaucracy, or the estates in civil society), along with the mediating institutions in civil society (the social estates, administration of justice, corporations, and public authority), all contribute to the overall *unity* of the modern state—where individual subjectivity and universal objectivity are finally, and unprecedentedly, reconciled.

Hic Rhodus, Hic Saltus: The Future

The modern state, therefore, is not just any state; it is the last link in the chain of *Weltgeist*. In his *Lectures on the Philosophy of History*, Hegel submits that for a state to be considered structurally sound and internally vigorous it must reconcile particular interests with its own universal interests; citizens must have duties to the state as well as rights against it. And while friction with particular interests and displays of individual passions are inescapable, he posits that the "latter must be subjected to a long and rigorous process of discipline before the ultimate unity is achieved." However, once a state reaches this unity it "marks the most flourishing period in its history, when its virtue, strength, and prosperity are at their height."[94] It is precisely this height that the modern state has reached—at least in principle. The state that Hegel depicts in the *Philosophy of Right*, as one commentator writes, is "not a state of the future but the end of a past history."[95] To be sure, in the *Philosophy of Right* Hegel does propose a few changes that could be made in existing European states; however, "these are part of the latest completion of the idea of the modern state described" in the *Philosophy of Right*.[96] So, when Hegel considers the time in which he lives he does indeed see it as the apotheosis of history.[97] As Hegel himself puts it, "world history travels from east to west; for Europe is the absolute end of history, just as Asia is the beginning."[98]

But this end of history is but a relative one, even for Hegel. *Historical time* certainly does not come to a standstill with the birth of the modern world. History marches always *forward*, but this march forward is not explored by him. If historical change can be considered the sine qua non of Hegel's philosophy of history, then his unwillingness to consider further historical change in the future can likewise be considered the sine qua non of his political philosophy. This is not to say however that Hegel completely ignores the possibility of future development, but only that future development is not the concern of philosophy. Of the possibility of future development Hegel points to America. It is, he says, the "country of the future, and its world-historical importance has yet to be revealed in the ages which lie ahead." Populated with those who are "weary of the historical arsenal of old Europe," America must eventually "abandon the ground on which world history has hitherto been enacted" because, he continues, "what has taken place there up till now is but an echo of the Old World and the expression of an alien life."[99] But to speculate upon the ground on which America will enact its historical development, or how America will express its authentic life, does not concern Hegel. Since America is a "country of the future, it is of no interest to us here," he says, and this is because "prophesy is not the business of the philosopher."[100]

Hegel considers the task of philosophy as being retrospective rather than prospective.[101] Hegel makes this point very explicit toward the end of his preface to the *Philosophy of Right*, which contains some of his most famous and most quoted passages. That philosophy "cannot consist in teaching the state what it ought to be; it can only show how the state, the ethical universe, is to be understood," or that "it is just as absurd to fancy that a philosophy can transcend its contemporary world as it is to fancy that an individual can overleap his own age, jump over Rhodes," or that "when philosophy paints its grey in grey, then has a shape of life grown old," or finally that the "owl of Minerva spreads its wings only with the falling of dusk,"[102] are examples of the retrospective character of philosophy as understood by Hegel. Since philosophy concerns itself with the rational, its task is to apprehend the rational in the present and the actual, not the future and the hypothetical.[103] Besides, if we took its task as being prospective, it would always come up short because philosophy arrives too late; it arrives only when a form of life has matured enough for philosophy to grasp the truth within the actual. Philosophy can only sum up an age. This being the case, Hegel's philosophy is put in a strange position. As Avineri suitably points out, the "tragic irony of Hegel's dialectical apprehension of his world, means that while Hegel saw himself as comprehending the new world of post-1789 (or post-1815) Europe, this by itself meant that this new world, which Hegel heralded in his *Phenomenology*, is already reaching its maturity and is somehow, slowly but surely, on its way out."[104] The modern world is in principle complete, and Hegel's philosophy of history is the story of its long and painful journey toward completion. Since philosophy is retrospective, it must wait to ponder the future, it must wait until the future has become the past. Or as Adriaan Peperzak has it, "just as there was a long period of transition between Plato and Christ, so, too, is it possible that the state legitimized by Hegel will last for centuries; a new foundation is not yet in sight and cannot yet be philosophically thematized. The thinker has to wait to see what history gives him to think about."[105]

Thus, Hegel's political philosophy has an earnest patiency or persistent discipline about it; especially considering that his philosophy is about historical change and historical time, and uses what could be considered *future-oriented* terms: development (*Entwicklung* or *Bildung*), dialectical movement (*Dialektische Bewegung*), purposiveness (*Zwecklichkeit*), progress (*Fortschritt*), and so on. If not exclusively forward-looking, such terminology is at least pregnant with future implications, even though for Hegel they are only future-oriented retrospectively (i.e., progress up until now). Moreover, coupled with this somewhat conservative stance toward the future is his radical stance toward the past. Taking into account his belief in the pastness of the past (or the nonduplicability of the past) on the one hand, and his belief that philosophy is not suited for prospective thinking on the other, Hegel seems to allow very little room to maneuver for those who have less patience, less discipline, and maybe even less faith than did Hegel. And yet room to maneuver is exactly what some followers of Hegel needed when, in the midst of renewed social and political upheaval in the 1830s and 1840s, the present was found to exhibit fewer signs that the modern age was in fact complete (even in principle), and when the present seemed to be giving birth to yet another phase in world history, an industrial phase.

Hegel's insistence on refusing to deal with the future, which is certainly understandable and is a logical consequence of his philosophy, betrays yet again that the future had become a problem for modern political philosophy. And if the modes of time could be said to have been roughly contiguous in the premodern world, then a good illustration of the breakup of temporality into thematizable modes is found in Hegel's political philosophy. The modes of time were held together by the splendor of his retrospective vision, but then collapsed again into discrete and thematizable modes once the present, which is the pivot of his system, was seen to need help either in completing or in inaugurating the new epoch. Hegel's philosophical estate was divided among his followers largely according to *temporal* characteristics. As early as the 1820s the "Hegelian school evolved into recognizable accommodationist, reformist, and 'revolutionary' positions" depending on whether the "historical actualization of absolute Reason . . . was defined as a completed process, a partially completed process, or a future goal."[106] By the 1830s the accommodationist influence began to wane, while the reformist and revolutionary stance gained in strength and influence.[107] In the 1830s, the moderate reformist Eduard Gans would hold the position that the "final stage in the process of reason's actualization had begun during the period of the French Revolution and Napoleonic reforms, and could thus be comprehended by Hegel, but the *process was not yet complete*."[108] In the words of another moderate, Karl Michelet, the "owl of Minerva yields to the cockcrow that announces the dawn of a new day."[109] August von Cieszkowski represents an even more radical position with regard to the future when in the late 1830s he argues that the "totality of history must consist of the past and of the future, of the road already travelled as well as of the road yet to be travelled, and hence our first task is the cognition of the essence of the *future* through speculation." In his philosophy of history, as Cieszkowski reads it, Hegel gave way to a negative prejudice which however natural and valid it may seem was no less an obstacle to proper comprehension. In his work he did not mention the *future* by name at all and he was even of the *opinion* that in exploring history philosophy can be only valid retrospectively and that the future should be completely excluded from the sphere of speculation. The position which we, on the other hand, affirm in advance is that without the *knowability of the future*, unless one conceives of the future as an integral part of history where the destiny of mankind is realized, it is impossible to know the organic, ideal totality and the apodictic process of world history. For this reason the establishment of the knowability of the future is an essential *precondition* for the organic structure of history.[110]

The reworking of Hegel's philosophy of history by Cieszkowski was motivated by religious concerns, but by the late 1830s and early 1840s a significant group of Left Hegelians began the process of secularizing Hegel's philosophy through a humanistic inversion.[111]

With the shift from religious concerns to humanistic ones, the point of contention became less about Hegelian inheritance than about Hegelian transcendence.[112] As one scholar aptly puts it, "less than a generation separates the philosophers who wept at Hegel's funeral from the Revolutionaries of 1848. Yet in this short period the Hegelians moved from contemplation to activity, from *theoria* to deed, and from theology to social and political concerns."[113] In this short time the modern world appeared to lurch forward, and for many it was no longer possible to philosophize in the manner of Hegel. If this new generation moved from contemplation to activity, it also shifted the emphasis away from the modern state and toward modern economics. At least this is what one of the most famous of this generation sought to do, when, in 1843, he observed that "the system of industry and trade, of ownership and exploitation of people" is leading to a "rupture within present-day society."[114]

Notes

1. *Hegel's Phenomenology of Spirit*, trans. A. V. Miller (Oxford: Oxford University Press, 1977), 6–7 (paras. 11 and 12).

2. For an explication of this dialectical progression see Duncan Forbes's summary in his introduction to Hegel's *Lectures on the Philosophy of World History* (Cambridge, Cambridge University Press, 1995), xvii. See also Burleigh Taylor Wilkins's *Hegel's Philosophy of History* (Ithaca, N.Y.: Cornell University Press, 1974), 28; and George Dennis O'Brien's *Hegel on Reason and History* (Chicago: University of Chicago Press, 1975), chapt. 2.

3. Hegel, *Lectures on the Philosophy of World History*, 12.

4. Hegel, *Lectures on the Philosophy of World History*, 13.

5. Hegel, *Lectures on the Philosophy of World History*, 12.

6. Hegel, *Lectures on the Philosophy of World History*, 14.

7. Hegel, *Lectures on the Philosophy of World History*, 16.

8. Forbes, "Introduction," in *Lectures on the Philosophy of World History*, xviii.

9. Hegel, *Lectures on the Philosophy of World History*, 17. Hegel here uses the Roman historian Livy as an example. Incidently, according to the editor this passage is a loose rendering of a few lines from Goethe's *Faust*: "The spirit of the times, I've long suspected,/Is but the spirit of the men—that's all—/In which the times they prate of are reflected."

10. Hegel, *Lectures on the Philosophy of World History*, 18.

11. Hegel denotes the latter as pragmatic history, which is a subcategory of reflective history.

12. Hegel, *Lectures on the Philosophy of World History*, 21.

13. Hegel, *Lectures on the Philosophy of World History*, 21.

14. Hegel, *Lectures on the Philosophy of World History*, 21. This aspect of Hegel's philosophy of history is, according to Jürgen Habermas, a central feature of "modernity's consciousness of time." Habermas, *The Philosophical Discourse of Modernity*, trans. Frederick G. Lawrence (Cambridge, Mass.: MIT Press, 1987), 1–22; see especially page 7 for his exploration of the idea that modernity is forced to "create its normativity out of itself."

15. Hegel, *Lectures in the Philosophy of World History*, 24.

16. If history for Hegel can be seen as "Spirit emptied out into Time," as he says in the *Phenomenology* (492, para. 808), then *historical development* is but the movement of Spirit through a succession of externalizations toward fulfillment.

17. Hegel, *Philosophy of Right*, trans. T. M. Knox (Oxford: Oxford University Press, 1967), 218 (para. 347).

18. Hegel, *Lectures on the Philosophy of World History*, 56.

19. Hegel, *Lectures on the Philosophy of World History*, 32.

20. Hegel, *Lectures on the Philosophy of World History*, 68–69 and 32. That Hegel had a profound appreciation for a melancholic view of the transient quality of history can hardly be doubted. Observations such as the ones quoted here are found throughout his study of world history.

21. More like a temporary reprieve since even philosophy cannot counter the cyclical nature of the cosmos.

22. Hegel, *Lectures on the Philosophy of World History*, 32. As an aside, the "positive" side of change is not merely offered as some kind of philosophical consolation to those who suffer the very real consequences of change, because as Hegel rather eloquently explains in *Lectures on the Philosophy of World History*, 67:

> What is usually called reality is seen by philosophy as no more than an idle semblance which has no reality in and for itself. If we have the impression that the events of the past are totally calamitous and devoid of sense, we can find consolation, so to speak, in this awareness. But consolation is merely something received in compensation for a misfortune which ought never to have happened in the first place, and it belongs to the world of finite things. Philosophy, therefore, is not really a means of consolation. It is more than that, for it transfigures reality with all its apparent injustices and reconciles it with the rational.

23. Hegel, *Lectures on the Philosophy of World History*, 125.

24. Hegel, *Lectures on the Philosophy of World History*, 125.

25. Hegel, *Lectures on the Philosophy of World History*, 125.

26. Hegel, *Lectures on the Philosophy of World History*, 126.

27. Hegel, *Lectures on the Philosophy of World History*, 126.

28. Hegel, *Lectures on the Philosophy of World History*, 61.

29. Hegel, *Lectures on the Philosophy of World History*, 61.

30. Hegel, *Lectures on the Philosophy of World History*, 125. The combination of both the quantitative and qualitative can be seen in the following passage in Hegel's *Phenomenology of Spirit*: "Just as the first breath drawn by a child after its long, quiet nourishment breaks the gradualness of merely quantitative growth—there is a qualitative leap, and the child is born" (6, para. 11).

31. Hegel, *Lectures on the Philosophy of World History*, 126.

32. Hegel, *Lectures on the Philosophy of World History*, 126–27.

33. Both dimensions are but two *moments* in the same process of development. The development of the former is explicated by Hegel in his *Phenomenology of Spirit*, and if we pause here to consider the underlying essence of this work, it is only to connect better the objective dimension (our major concern here) with its subjective counterpart.

34. Hegel, *Phenomenology of Spirit*, 111–19 (paras. 178–96).

35. It is important to note that for Hegel the category of labor is not simply a specific form of the experience of consciousness, but an indispensable formative activity (which describes the essential activity of Spirit) whereby natural consciousness is overcome by transforming external nature (the other) into something that reflects the subject. The labor process presented in the dialectic of lordship and bondage, in other words, is the dynamic process which underlies the whole of the *phenomenology* of spirit, writ small. In this way, one can distinguish between the labor process presented by Hegel at the specific or microlevel (the labor of the bondsman), and labor process as a metacategory in Hegel's overall system.

36. Hegel, *Lectures on the Philosophy of World History*, 129.

37. Hegel, *Lectures on the Philosophy of World History*, 197. Just so that there is no confusion, a nation and a state are intimately connected in that the will of a *nation* manifests itself or expresses itself in the *state*. Or to follow Forbes, "the state is the 'overreaching' universal, which both needs and makes possible the particularity of the *Volk*, the unique culture of the 'nation.'" "Introduction," xxvi.

38. Hegel, *Lectures on the Philosophy of World History*, 135.

39. Hegel, *Lectures on the Philosophy of World History*, 135.

40. Hegel, *Lectures on the Philosophy of World History*, 136.

41. Hegel, *Lectures on the Philosophy of World History*, 136. Hegel contrasts the need of the state to create a "memory" or a past of itself with the emotion of love, and with religious contemplation, and argues that these are "wholly immediate and satisfying in themselves; but the external existence of the state, despite the rational laws and principles it contains, is an incomplete present which cannot understand itself and develop an integrated consciousness without reference to the past."

42. Hegel, *Lectures on the Philosophy of World History*, 134.

43. Hegel, *Lectures on the Philosophy of World History*, 134 and 137. This attitude is notable not only because it is taken up by an idealist philosopher, but also because it indicates how important actual, empirical history had become in considering the past.

44. Hegel, *Lectures on the Philosophy of World History*, 136.

45. Hegel, *Lectures on the Philosophy of World History*, 137.

46. Hegel, *Lectures on the Philosophy of World History*, 145.

47. Here Hegel is following Aristotle in his *De Mundo*, trans. E. S. Forster (Oxford: Clarendon Press, 1914), where Aristotle links Κρόνος with Χρόνος.

48. Hegel, *Lectures on the Philosophy of World History*, 145.

49. Hegel, *Lectures on the Philosophy of World History*, 145.

50. Hegel, *Lectures on the Philosophy of World History*, 146.

51. Hegel, *Lectures on the Philosophy of World History*, 146.

52. Hegel, *Lectures on the Philosophy of World History*, 146.

53. Hegel, *Lectures on the Philosophy of World History*, 147.

54. Hegel, *Lectures on the Philosophy of World History*, 61. My italics.

55. Hegel, Likewise, "if we wish to treat history philosophically," says Hegel, "we must avoid such expressions as 'this state would not have collapsed if there had been someone who . . .' etc." Hegel, *Lectures on the Philosophy of World History*, 52.

56. Hegel, *Lectures on the Philosophy of World History*, 53.

57. Hegel, *Lectures on the Philosophy of World History*, 120.

58. Hegel, *Lectures on the Philosophy of World History*, 129.

59. Hegel, *Lectures on the Philosophy of World History*, 129–30.

60. Hegel, *Lectures on the Philosophy of World History*, 46. It is important to stress, as does Forbes, that "if the task of the philosopher is to think experience concretely and to describe the given, the philosophy of history cannot be an *a priori* scheme, thought out prior to observation of the facts and the work of the historian as such. The *Geist* of modern man, his claim to freedom, is real enough, and must have come about in history." Forbes, "Introduction," xxiii. And Hegel sees his task as inter alia one of reconstruction to show how freedom developed in history.

61. Hegel, *Lectures on the Philosophy of History*, 46.

62. Hegel, *Lectures on the Philosophy of World History*, 197. Hegel defines substantial freedom here as the "implicit rationality of the will which is subsequently developed in the state" which exists where subjective freedom is underdeveloped or where it is not allowed expression, and where "commandments and laws are regarded as firmly established in and for themselves, and the individual subject adopts an attitude of complete subservience towards them."

63. Ultimate reconciliation is what Charles Taylor aptly describes as the "fullness of moral autonomy, with the recovery of . . . community." *Hegel* (Cambridge: Cambridge University Press, 1975), 365. For a comprehensive account of this well-known though often misunderstood aspect of Hegel's political philosophy, see Michael O. Hardimon's *Hegel's Social Philosophy: The Project of Reconciliation* (Cambridge: Cambridge University Press, 1994).

64. Hegel, *Lectures on the Philosophy of World History*, 196–209. Again, these objective phases in the development of spirit have subjective correlates in the evolution of consciousness, which is the focus of Hegel's *Phenomenology of Spirit*.

65. Hegel, *Lectures on the Philosophy of World History*, 197.

66. *Old age* here meaning strong and mature.

67. Hegel, *Lectures on the Philosophy of World History*, 151.

68. Robert C. Solomon, *In the Spirit of Hegel* (Oxford: Oxford University Press, 1983), 42.

69. Cited by Solomon's *In the Spirit of Hegel*, ix.

70. Some years later, for example, Hegel still holds the position that "a new epoch has arisen in the world." *Hegel's Lectures on the History of Philosophy*, vol. 3, trans. E. S. Haldane and Frances H. Simson (London: Routledge & Kegan Paul, 1955), 551.

71. Hegel, *Lectures on the Philosophy of World History*, 32.

72. Manfred Riedel, *Between Tradition and Revolution: The Hegelian Transformation of Political Philosophy*, trans. Walter Wright (Cambridge: Cambridge University Press, 1984), 142. Riedel uses the word *application* here in the technical hermeneutical sense (as a "traditional essential moment in hermeneutics") as expounded by Hans-Georg Gadamer in his *Truth and Method*.

73. Hegel, *Lectures on the Philosophy of World History*, 95.

74. Hegel, *Philosophy of Right*, 86 (para. 129).

75. This conclusion emerges from the dialectical stage of development (in essence a critique of Kantian ethics) where the moral will attempts a subjective reconciliation with the universal that ultimately falters because the objective world fails to reflect the subjective reconciliation. As a result the moral will continually feels alienated in its attempt to measure up to its *oughts*, which are abstract and formed independently from reality. It is only when, Hegel argues, the "identity of the good with the subjective will [emerges], an identity which therefore is concrete and the truth of them both" do we enter the stage of a true ethical life where "the *objective order* . . . comes on the scene in place of the good in the abstract." *Philosophy of Right*, 103 and 105 (paras. 141 and 144). My italics.

76. Hardimon, *Hegel's Social Philosophy: The Project of Reconciliation*, 34.

77. Hegel, *Philosophy of Right*, 109 (para. 153 and para. 154).

78. Hegel, *Philosophy of Right*, 123 (para. 185). "[A]s soon as reflection supervened and individuals withdrew into themselves and dissociated themselves from established custom to live their own lives according to their own wishes, degeneration and contradiction arose." Hegel, *Lectures on the Philosophy of World History*, 62.

79. Hegel, *Lectures on the Philosophy of World History*, 62.

80. Hegel, *Philosophy of Right*, 83 (para. 124).

81. For a conceptual history of the term *civil society*, see Jean L. Cohen and Andrew Arato's *Civil Society and Political Theory* (Cambridge, Mass.: MIT Press, 1992), 83–116.

82. Cohen and Arato, *Civil Society and Political Theory*, 91.

83. For an in-depth look at this conceptual feat see Riedel's chapter "'State' and 'Civil Society': Linguistic Context and Historical Origin," in *Between Tradition and Revolution: The Hegelian Transformation of Political Philosophy*, 129–56. It should also be noted that Hegel's understanding of civil society includes within its domain not only the economic life of the community (system of needs), but also the institutions of social estates or classes (*Stände*) and the administration of justice, corporations, and public authority (policing).

84. Hegel, *Philosophy of Right*, 109 (para. 154).

85. Hegel, *Philosophy of Right*, 266–67 (addition to para. 182).

86. Hegel, *Philosophy of Right*, 122–23 (para. 182).

87. Hegel, *Philosophy of Right*, 123 (para. 183).

88. Hegel, *Philosophy of Right*, 126 (para. 189). Or more explicitly stated, "subjective self-seeking turns into a contribution to the satisfaction of the needs of everyone else. That is to say, by a dialectical advance, subjective self-seeking turns into the mediation of the particular through the universal, with the result that each man in earning, producing, and enjoying on his own account is *eo ipso* producing and earning for the enjoyment of everyone else." Hegel, *Philosophy of Right*, 129–30 (para. 199).

89. Hardimon, *Hegel's Social Philosophy: The Project of Reconciliation*, 190.

90. Hegel, *Philosophy of Right*, 123 (para. 185).

91. Shlomo Avineri, *Hegel's Theory of the Modern State* (Cambridge: Cambridge University Press, 1972), 146–47.

92. The principle of the modern state is what Hegel considers in the *Philosophy of Right*, and this should not be construed to designate a particular, existing state. As Hardimon writes, "it is now generally recognized that Hegel was not the friend of the Prussian restoration he was once taken to be." *Hegel's Social Philosophy: The Project of Reconciliation*, 27.

93. Hegel, *Philosophy of Right*, 161 (para. 260).

94. Hegel, *Lectures on the Philosophy of World History*, 73.

95. Adriaan Th. Peperzak, *Philosophy and Politics: A Commentary on the Preface to Hegel's Philosophy of Right* (Dordrecht: Martinus Nijhoff, 1987), 117–18.

96. Peperzak, *Philosophy and Politics*, 117. For a look at Hegel's support of certain reform measures (in practice) see Hardimon, *Hegel's Social Philosophy: The Project of Reconciliation*, 26ff.

97. Avineri, *Hegel's Theory of the Modern State*, 129.

98. Hegel, *Lectures on the Philosophy of World History*, 197.

99. Hegel, *Lectures on the Philosophy of World History*, 170–71. See also his addition to page 170.

100. Hegel, *Lectures on the Philosophy of World History*, 171.

101. Wilkins, *Hegel's Philosophy of History*, 82–84.

102. Hegel, *Philosophy of Right*, 11 and 13.

103. Hegel, *Philosophy of Right*, 10. Since this touches upon Hegel's position that "what is rational is actual and what is actual is rational," it is important to note that what is *actual* should not be equated with what simply exists or with what exists factually. As Peperzak explains, "actuality does not include everything which just happens to exist. Primary *experience*, in which all kinds of things appear, demands a consideration which distinguishes between the merely ephemeral and meaningless on the one hand, and the important and meaningful which remains the same and is eternal on the other. Hegel calls the former *appearance* (*Erscheinung*), in which he not only includes the contingent, but also forms of evil, such as 'error' and 'every decadent existence.' (Encyclopaedia, C. 6A.) *Actuality* (*Wirklichkeit*) is only that reality which is as good as it should be, the necessity of which can be understood by a thoroughgoing reason and which is thus necessarily good." Peperzak, *Philosophy and Politics*, 94–95.

104. Avineri, *Hegel's Theory of the Modern State*, 129.

105. Peperzak, *Philosophy and Politics*, 117.

106. John Edward Toews, *Hegelianism: The Path toward Dialectical Humanism, 1805–1841* (Cambridge: Cambridge University Press, 1980), 7–8.

107. Toews, *Hegelianism*, 205 and 223.

108. Toews, *Hegelianism*, 230. My italics.

109. *Jahrbücher für wissenschaftliche Kritik* (1831), pt. 1, col. 697. Cited in Toews, *Hegelianism*, 232.

110. "Prolegomena to Historiosophy," in *Selected Writings of August Cieszkowski*, ed. and trans. André Liebich (Cambridge: Cambridge University Press, 1979), 51–52.

111. In his preface to *Principles of the Philosophy of the Future* (note the title), Ludwig Feuerbach writes that the "philosophy of the future has the task of leading philosophy from the realm of 'departed souls' back into the realm of embodied and living souls; of pulling philosophy down from the divine, self-sufficient bliss in the realm of ideas into human misery." *Principles of the Philosophy of the Future*, trans. Manfred Vogel (Indianapolis: Hackett, 1986), 3.

112. Left Hegelianism generally held the position that "moderates had chosen to take their stand with a dying culture and had become the sterile caretakers of a metaphysical system that had lost its ability to reconcile man with his historical world." Toews, *Hegelianism*, 235.

113. André Liebich, *Between Ideology and Utopia: The Politics and Philosophy of August Cieszkowski* (Dordrecht: Reidel, 1979), 20.

114. Karl Marx, "Letters from the *Deutsch-Französische Jahrbücher*," in *Collected Works*, vol. 3 (New York: International Publishers, 1975), 141.

Chapter Four

Jumping Over Rhodes: Marx

Philosophers Have Only Interpreted the World . . .

One could hardly find a better example of the conviction that the modern world was pregnant with a future new life than in the work of Marx; and few perceived, as did Marx, the dialectical problem of past and future within modernity as clearly. His political philosophy is a philosophy of modernity. That he can be considered a philosopher of modernity should come as no great surprise, not the least because, as Göran Therborn brings to our attention,

> in the first eight pages of the *Werke* edition of Marx's and Engels's *Communist Manifesto* we learn about "modern industry" (three times), "modern bourgeois society" (twice), the "modern bourgeoisie" (twice), "modern workers" (twice), and once about "modern state power," "modern productive forces," and "modern relations of production." And Marx's "ultimate purpose" (*letzte Endzweck*) of *Capital* was to "disclose the economic law of motion of modern society," as he put it in his preface to the first edition.[1]

We can distill from his lifework as a philosopher of modernity a profound commentary on the dynamics of modern temporality. In his writings the modern world is portrayed as that which stands between a past full of human misery and a future full of human promise, between prehistory and true human history, and the modern world is accordingly conceptualized by Marx as exhibiting both misery and promise, both despair and hope. Portraying the modern world as being suffused with its contrary—a humanity reduced to the cash-nexus, on the one hand, and a humanity on the threshold of true human emancipation, on the other—Marx observed and gave expression to what Therborn calls the "two horns of modernity, the emancipatory and the exploitative."[2] Marx provides a brief sketch of this in a speech he delivered in 1856, which is worth a lengthy quote:

There is one great fact, characteristic of this our 19th century, a fact which no party dares deny. On the one hand, there have started into life industrial and scientific forces, which no epoch of the former human history had ever suspected. On the other hand, there exists symptoms of decay, far surpassing the horrors recorded of the latter times of the Roman empire. In our days, everything seems pregnant with its contrary. Machinery, gifted with the wonderful power of shortening and fructifying human labor, we behold starving and overworking it. The new-fangled sources of wealth, by some strange weird spell, are turned into sources of want. The victories of art seem bought by the loss of character. At the same pace that mankind masters nature, man seems to become enslaved to other men or to his own infamy. Even the pure light of science seems unable to shine but on the dark background of ignorance. All our invention and progress seem to result in endowing material forces with intellectual life, and in stultifying human life into a material force. This antagonism between modern industry and science on the one hand, modern misery and dissolution on the other hand; this antagonism between the productive powers, and the social relations of our epoch is a fact, palpable, overwhelming, and not to be controverted.[3]

Being pregnant with its contrary, moreover, the modern world shows unmistakable signs of instability and discontinuity, or, to put it another way (and to use a phrase borrowed from Marx and made familiar by Marshall Berman), in the modern world *all that is solid melts into air*. In this same volcanic speech Marx declares that there are those "who are as much the invention of modern time as machinery itself" and it is they who know the "shrewd spirit that continues to mark all these contradictions." It is, he says, "Robin Goodfellow, the old mole that can work in the earth so fast, that worthy pioneer—the Revolution."[4] For Marx, the revolutions of 1848, although in effect only "small fractures and fissures in the dry crust of European society," signaled the beginning of a revolt if only by symbolically denouncing the abyss which the modern world had quickly become.[5] Continuing his geologic metaphor Marx comments that the foundations upon which the modern world rests, while appearing quite solid, were exposed by the revolutions of 1848 as actually quite unstable and volatile; what the revolutions exposed was that "beneath the apparently solid surface, they [the revolutions] betrayed oceans of liquid matter, only needing expansion to rend into fragments continents of hard rock. Nosily and confusedly they proclaimed the emancipation of the Proletariat, *i.e.* the secret of the nineteenth century."[6]

We consult this speech less to display Marx's rhetorical dexterity, which is extraordinary, than to introduce his understanding of modernity. The phenomenal advances in industry and science which, as he says, no former epoch could have even predicted, are to be contrasted with concomitant and unprecedented exploitation, generalized poverty, and spiritual impoverishment of the majority of humans. With such basic contradictions Marx believed that this condition could not continue and should be viewed instead as a time of transition—an exploitative past is giving way to nothing less than an emancipated future. Marx, as a philosopher of modernity, can be considered more specifically as a philosopher of this transitional time, a philosopher of modern social revolution. And when Marx writes that the "social revolution of the nineteenth century cannot create its poetry from the past but only from the future,"[7] he exemplifies a typically modern view of the past (that which can be and continually is superseded) and the future (that which can be shaped as we see fit). But for Marx forging a future that is decidedly different and decidedly better than the past demands not a belief in an ever-expanding progress, not a belief in the unfolding of spirit; it demands instead a radical future orientation, and formative revolutionary activity informed by a future-oriented consciousness.

The stress on future-oriented revolutionary activity is clearly evident when Marx uses, as did Hegel (albeit with a different emphasis), the passage "Hic Rhodus, Hic Salta!/Hier ist die Rose, hier tanze!"[8] Unlike Hegel, who uses the passage to warn political philosophers against searching for ideals beyond the present, Marx uses it to exhort the workers to march beyond the present. While Hegel stands in the present with his back to the future and his eyes cast upon the present and *its past*, Marx stands in the present with his back to the past and his eyes cast upon the present and *its future*. Such an interpretation fits well with Marx's most celebrated statement on revolutionary action: "The philosophers have only *interpreted* the world in different ways; the point is to *change* it."[9] However, his eleventh thesis is deceptive in its simplicity even for Marx. To change the world and to command the future, an understanding of the dynamic relation between the past, the present, and the future is necessary.

Cannot Just Leap into the Future

The relevance of temporality is stated best in a letter from Marx to Arnold Ruge in September of 1843. The letter begins with a comment on the question of where to establish their prospective journal, the *Deutsch-Französische Jahrbücher*. In an earlier correspondence Ruge had stated that he wanted to establish the journal in one of the old cities of Europe, but then he later agreed with Marx that an old city may prove inappropriate, and now in the September letter Marx comments: "I am glad you have made up your mind and, ceasing to look at the past, are turning your thoughts ahead to a new enterprise. And so—to Paris, to the old university of philosophy—*absit omen*—and the new capital of the new world!"[10] The journal was to provide a new venue, a "new rallying point" for independent thinkers and, with its inception, had many obstacles to surmount.[11] Marx recognized that more than any external obstacle to a successful rallying point were internal ones largely because while "no doubt exists on the question of 'Whence', all the greater confusion prevails on the question of 'Whither.'"[12] In other words, while the *past* has been more or less uniformly and unflatteringly deciphered by those who wish to change the world, the question of what path to take into the *future* remained confused.[13] This confusion was not due to a dearth of material regarding the future, but rather due to the contradictory positions about the future that were conjured by the imaginations of late-eighteenth- and early-nineteenth-century writers and their enthusiasts. What is most distressing, Marx adds, is that "not only has a state of general anarchy set in among the reformers, but everyone will have to admit to himself that he has no exact idea what the future ought to be."[14] If this were true, however, it certainly did not stop the reformers from thinking and writing about it.

While there may have been much confusion around the issue of *where to*, it was impossible for Marx not to notice a radically new emphasis on the future since at least the time of the Enlightenment—an emphasis which especially permeates the utopian thought of the late eighteenth and early nineteenth centuries. When Marx and Engels first formed their lifelong association in the early 1840s, they indeed "mounted a stage literally swarming with utopian systems."[15] Moreover, unlike premodern utopian systems, these were explicitly future-oriented systems and were designed to help guide the creation of a completely new political, economic, and social order. These future-oriented utopian systems were different from their premodern counterparts in that prior to the changed experiential condition that was opened up with the emergence of modernity, when expectations were to a large degree limited by past experiences, utopian thought usually projected ideals into a past Golden Age, or situated ideals within historical cycles, or contained the boundaries of the future within the Last Judgment of Christian eschatology. Even early modern utopian thought was not future-oriented. For example, the utopias of Thomas More and Tommaso Campanella are *spatially* located in some imaginary present, not *temporally* located in the future. More's ideal commonwealth is reported—by the fictitious Portuguese mariner, Raphael Hythloday—to be located in a far-off island. As reported by another mariner—this time a Genoese sea captain—Campanella's city of the sun is located in Taprobane (Ceylon).[16] What makes the utopian thought of someone like More modern is not that it is radically future-oriented but that it is radically humanistic. As J. C. Davis explains, More's utopia suggests that there is a "conceivable social ideal in which fallible humans live in a society of moral dignity and worth without the aid of revelation," which can be devised and created "without benefit of divine agency."[17] However, to do so, Davis continues, More "had to think through some of the fundamental issues of politics, but not all of them. For, while he had to work *with* fallible human material, he did not have to work *through* it," and the result "was a work of supreme artifice: the creation of an artificial island by manual excavation."[18] Such a feat did extract utopia from the grip of the past, but it also extracted utopia from time itself.

The late eighteenth century however saw a fundamental shift in the form of utopia away from an unsurpassable past, away from an imaginary present, and toward a future *in this world*. Historians of utopia normally locate this shift with the publication of Louis-Sabastien Mercier's *L'An 2440* in 1771.[19] It was Mercier who, by placing his utopia in Paris, France, in the distant year 2440, brought future-time into focus. Using as an epigraph a line from Leibniz which tells us that the "present is pregnant with the future," Mercier gave expression, as Kumar puts it, to the "new zest for the future which in the second half of the eighteenth century was transforming both the form and the substance of utopia."[20] However, regardless of who receives credit for initiating the shift, there can be little doubt that the late eighteenth and early nineteenth centuries saw the proliferation of explicitly future-oriented utopias. Unlike in premodern utopias, the coupling of utopia with a temporalized history allowed modern ideal conceptions to become part of the historical process. In a specifically modern tone, for example, Henri Saint-Simon writes that the "imagination of poets has placed the Golden Age in the infancy of the human race, amidst the ignorance and coarseness of ancient times," yet they are mistaken. "It would have been much better to consign the iron age there" because, he continues, "the Golden Age of the human race is not behind us; it lies before us, in the perfection of the social order. Our fathers did not see it; our children will arrive there one day; it is for us to clear the way."[21] Modern utopian thought, then, valorizes the future at the expense of the past. Saint-Simon, Charles Fourier, and Robert Owen were "intoxicated with the future," and for them the "past was a mere prologue and the present a spiritual and moral, even a physical, burden that at times was well-nigh unendurable."[22] With slight variations the future became the repository of human hopes that could be planned and carried out by human action.

So, when Marx observed that confusion prevailed on the question of *where to* he certainly was not exaggerating. The early years of post-Enlightenment optimism, or, as one commentator puts it, of "faith in unbounded progress through the application of human reasoning,"[23] saw a proliferation of modern future-oriented projects including but not limited to the modern utopian systems. In other words, Marx was not the only one seeking to change the world. His understanding of modernity, with its problems and potentials, and his vision of the future had to compete and contend with many other visions. In the midst of numerous calls to change the world, Marx found it necessary to clear away some of the confusion. The first attempt to do so is found in the third section of the *Manifesto of the Communist Party*, written in 1848.[24]

Although brief and lacking in detail, this third section classifies and criticizes various rivals whose visions were bandied about in the early part of the nineteenth century, each with its peculiar critique of the present, and each with its unique prescription for the future. Though not explicitly expressed by Marx, his classification considers each different vision around the issue of temporality. Among the various wishes to change the world there are a few stragglers whose visions, while clothed in modern garb, are products of nostalgic yearning of times past (feudal socialism and petty-bourgeois socialism); and there are some who, although they reject the temptation to return to past political and economic structures, are nevertheless blinded by the brilliance of the present and only wish to change the unfortunate side-effects of modern capitalist society (bourgeois socialism); and finally there are those (with whom Marx has a certain affinity) who reject the past and the present and desire to go forward into a newly wrought future (utopian socialism).

While Marx combines together the more future-oriented thinkers with the nonfuture-oriented ones under the same general heading, he clearly heaps more scorn on the latter. One distinctly nonfuture-oriented vision considered by Marx is put forward by the aristocracy. According to Marx, the aristocracy was no longer in a position to seriously challenge the political power of modern bourgeois society, and consequently, only a war of words was possible for them. The remnants of the feudal aristocracy wrote political pamphlets that condemned modern bourgeois society, while at the same time argued for a restored monarchy. However, to garner sympathy and support, and possibly to appear more timely, they advanced their vision in the name of the exploited working class, whom they sought to enlist as allies in their indictment of bourgeois society. The aristocracy, writes Marx, "took their revenge by singing lampoons on their new master, and whispering in his ears sinister prophecies of coming catastrophe."[25] The solutions put forth by the aristocracy include a somewhat haphazard collection of old feudal attitudes and new socialistic positions which Marx characterizes as "half lamentation, half lampoon, half echo of the past, half menace of the future," and while "striking the bourgeoisie at its very core through bitter, witty, biting judgements," their ultimate cause strikes Marx as comical because of a "total incapacity to grasp the course of modern history."[26] A similar reproach is leveled against another nonfuture-oriented vision advanced by the petty-bourgeoisie. As Marx explains, the "feudal aristocracy is not the only class that was ruined by the bourgeoisie" and is "not the only class whose conditions of life withered and died in modern bourgeois society."[27] Petty-bourgeois socialism exhibits a similar mixture of the old with the new with the aim of restoring a life, which, in Marx's opinion, has become an irretrievable part of the past. Such a vision wishes to turn back time by restoring the "traditional means of production and trade" or even more magically by forcing "modern means of production and trade back into the confines of traditional property relations that are now being—and must be—dismantled."[28] Either way, Marx concludes, such a position is "reactionary and utopian in equal measure."[29]

A final nonfuture-oriented vision considered by Marx is one that is described as purely reformist. Advocates of this type of vision (the list includes bourgeois "economists, philanthropists, humanitarians, do-gooders for the working classes, charity organizers, animal welfare enthusiasts, temperance union workers, [and] two-a-penny reformers of multifarious kinds") genuinely wish to "redress *social grievances*" but they do not wish to return to past political and economic structures in order to do so.[30] But neither do they wish to challenge the present-day bourgeois order. For them the present-day world is close to being the best of possible worlds, and some tinkering here and there is all that is required for a more perfect world. They wish for reform, Marx argues, but only to secure and maintain bourgeois society. As Marx sees it, the reformers "want the living conditions of modern society without the struggles and dangers necessarily arising from it. They want existing society with the exception of the revolutionary elements bent on destroying it." In short, "they want the bourgeoisie without the proletariat."[31]

Hence, in this third section Marx recognizes that while there were many calls to change the world, not all wished to change the world into something completely new. In the name of a better future some have proposed a cleverly disguised return to the past, and some a more charitable present. Only proponents of critical-utopian socialism and communism were antagonistic to both the past and the present. It is only they who felt a thorough and radical restructuring of the world was necessary. Marx groups together the modern utopians Saint-Simon, Fourier, and Owen as founders of this truly future-oriented vision. It is no accident that they are considered together; the idea that these three formed a "utopian trinity" was commonplace by the 1830s.[32] Marx used a broad brush with which to paint his critique of the utopian socialists; and while he is not known for his constructive criticism, he is rather charitable in his overall assessment. His critical stance toward the utopian socialists takes shape around a simple position, the position that "critical-utopian socialism and communism stand in inverse relationship to historical development."[33] From this vantage point the utopian socialists exhibit the mark of having emerged at an early stage of modern capitalist development, and thus their perceptions and prescriptions—while important—are fatefully underdeveloped and premature.

This is especially so with regard to modern class conflict. The utopian socialists were perceptive enough to "see the conflict between classes as well as the active elements of dissolution in prevailing society itself."[34] Moreover, their prescriptions for radical change offered not only to remedy class conflict, but to remedy class conflict largely in support of the working class. However, what the utopian socialists failed to perceive was that class conflict is intimately connected and moves in tandem with the growth of industry, and without this insight they failed to uncover the "material conditions for the emancipation of the proletariat," and what is worse, especially when they move from theory to practice, they "discern on the side of the proletariat no historical autonomy, no political movement of its own."[35] In other words, they were unable to see that modern capitalism was in the process of producing its own gravediggers, as Marx writes earlier in the *Manifesto*, or that modern capitalism was in the process of producing the material weapons of philosophy, as he writes in an earlier work.[36] True, they had the working-class interests at heart; however, they focused on the proletariat less because they saw the emancipatory potential of the working class, than because to them the working class represented the "class that suffers most."[37] To alleviate the suffering of the working class, the utopian socialists appeal to all of humanity. They acknowledge class conflict but they wish to situate themselves and their prescriptions outside the fray of class conflict. They simply do not see the potential class barriers to their proposals. In their eyes the nascent modern-class struggle can be mollified by general appeals to reason, and what is worse, appeals to the beneficence of the ruling class. Such appeals, Marx argues, are what make their proposals utopian in a negative sense. Every step of the way they disregard historical specificity and replace historical fact with fantasy, "in place of activity in society they have to introduce their personally invented forms of action, in place of historical conditions for emancipation of the proletariat they have to introduce fantastic ones, in place of the gradually developed organisation of the proletariat into a class they have to introduce a specially contrived organisation of society."[38] And finally they refuse to consider political engagement and revolutionary action as options; instead they wish to "reach their goal by peaceful means and seek through the power of example to pave the way for the new social Gospel through small-scale experiments, which naturally fail."[39] On the grand scale of historical change, they are politically impotent.

Since the past and present ills of human society need but a calm and orderly acceptance of their well-thought-out solutions, and since acceptance by force would be unacceptable for them, the utopian socialists have to resort to the power of persuasion—across class interests no less—by relying on the sheer brilliance of their vision. On this point Marx rather facetiously writes, "anyone needs but to understand their system in order to recognize it as the best possible plan for the best possible society."[40] Or as Marx writes a year earlier, they "want workers to leave the old society alone, the better to be able to enter the new society which they have prepared for them with so much foresight."[41] Having said this, however, Marx reveals a certain appreciation for the utopian socialists. They come on the scene, he writes, "in a time when the proletariat is still highly undeveloped and hence comprehending its own position in a fantastic way, [and therefore] these fantastic images of future society correspond to its first deeply felt urge for a general reorganisation of society."[42] But owing to the undeveloped nature of capitalism, the utopian socialists were too precipitous in their general pronouncements that class harmony was just on the horizon, and too naive in their presumption that all that was needed was to follow peacefully their well-laid plans.[43] Their prescriptions will not bring an end to class conflict; on the contrary, their prescriptions presuppose the end of class conflict. Nevertheless, the ideas of the utopian socialists are valuable because they are not only critical of the established order, "they attack all the fundamental principles of existing society."[44] Their efforts have furnished honorable and enlightened material for workers, and the working class movement, says Marx, owes a debt to these critical, if misguided, comrades.

But while the founders can get off lightly, their disciples cannot. The founders could not have foreseen the development of class struggle and they should not be held responsible for their lack of understanding; however, subsequent intensification of class conflict and the maturation of class struggle, Marx argues, should not have gone unnoticed by the disciples. Marx therefore has more patience with the founders, who were critical and revolutionary, than with their disciples: "Though the originators of these systems were revolutionary in many senses, their disciples have in every case formed reactionary sects." Their disciples, moreover, "still dream of an experimental realisation of their social utopias, the establishment of individual phalansteries, the foundation of home colonies, the building of a little Icaria—pocket editions of the new Jerusalem—and to erect all these castles in the air, they must appeal to the philanthropy of the bourgeois heart and purse."[45]

Marx's critique of the utopian socialists, here as elsewhere, certainly lacks the rigor characteristic of his many polemical exegeses. One can even call attention to a basic political motive behind the critique of the utopians, as Kumar evidently does when he writes that the rejection of utopian socialism by Marx and Engels stems from their attempt to "demonstrate that their kind of socialism was superior to the many other varieties currently on offer."[46] This is true. The *Manifesto* is after all a *political* document. However, as Marx sees it, he is not offering yet another system, or yet another vision of the future with the hope of dazzling the other varieties out of existence. Marx's stance stems not only from *political* considerations, but from *theoretical* ones as well. Marx did not need to provide a detailed refutation of the constituent parts that characterize the utopian socialists' vision of the future because from a purely theoretical standpoint their vision had only a tenuous connection to the specificity of the present. Marx's critique undercuts from the root. This is not to say that their vision of the future was merely fanciful or dreamlike or unrealistic, or that they are designated as utopian because their vision was *completely* disconnected from the present. They were a product of the *industrial-present*, and their vision of the future emerged as a response to the socioeconomic upheaval of the expanding industrialism of modern capitalism, and as such, Marx recognizes their important critical contributions—they are, after all, *critical*-utopians.[47] Instead this is to say that implied in Marx's critique of the utopian socialists is a variation of Hegel's idea of historical time—an Owl of Minerva that now is unafraid to glance forward.

If *time* emerged as the new focus in modern utopian thought, and if *future-time* became the most important thematic category, then for Marx mere *future orientation* is not enough. To be sure, their utopian systems are both modern and temporal; they presuppose that the future can be better than the past, and they assert that human activity—not divine activity—would bring about this better future. To a certain extent they even connect their vision with the forward flow of history—that which lies immediately in front of us. However, the utopian socialists fail to place a premium on temporal coordination; instead of placing their visions squarely within the modes of time, they attempt to *leap out of time*—out of the present and into the future. Their visions may be temporal, but their theoretical approaches are atemporal; thus there is little latitude for political action to construct a better future because their theories cannot be linked with actual political potentials in the present. The consequence of being disconnected from present human activity is that they do not go beyond the early modern utopias. From Marx's standpoint, their vision of the future is utopian in the sense that they presuppose the overcoming of class antagonisms, and the overcoming of class antagonisms presupposes present-day class struggle. Centuries of class oppression cannot be eliminated through the good graces of philanthropists or through the sheer weight of persuasion through meticulously prepared blueprints.

Indeed, the need to persuade humanity of their vision by assembling detailed blueprints for the future is a sure sign of the utopian socialists' political detachment from present-day class struggle. The notion that one can design a blueprint for the future and then make present reality somehow conform to it is anathema to Marx. In a certain sense blueprints require the creation of the future ex nihilo, and for Marx it is ridiculous to think that reality can be made to conform to a blueprint created out of the imagination. Marx is consistent on this point throughout his life. In 1843 Marx, in a sarcastic tone, writes that until now "philosophers have had the solution of all riddles lying in their writing-desks, and the stupid, exoteric world had only to open its mouth for the roast pigeons of absolute knowledge to fly in it."[48] Some thirty years later Marx scoffs at the reproach by one of his critics that he only looks into reality and does not provide recipes for the future: "Thus the Paris 'Revue Positiviste' reproaches me in that, on the one hand, I treat economics metaphysically, and on the other hand—imagine!—confine myself to the mere critical analysis of actual facts, instead of writing recipes (Comtist ones?) for the cook-shops of the future."[49] And while reflecting on the Paris Commune of 1870–1871 he contends that the "working class did not expect miracles from the Commune," and they did not have "ready-made utopias to introduce *par décret du peuple*." However, they did know, according to Marx, "that in order to work out their own emancipation, and along with it that higher form to which present society is irresistibly tending, by its own economic agencies, they will have to pass through long struggles, through a series of historic processes, transforming circumstances and men," and looking only to the present struggle at hand, "they have no ideas to realise, but to set free the elements of the new society with which old collapsing bourgeois society is itself pregnant."[50] This consistently held position, however, should not be interpreted as a prohibition on thinking about the future. Marx's criticism of the utopian socialists rests not on their anticipatory thinking *per se*, but instead rests on their inability to connect it to historical time. As Draper puts it, for Marx "utopianism was *that way* of thinking which makes the future an arbitrary isolate,"[51] or as Vincent Geoghegan rightly observes, for Marx the "issue is not the future versus the present, but that the future be grounded in the present."[52]

The utopian socialists were simply too captivated with the future, and what was needed was a sober look at present reality. If it be true that the present is pregnant with its future, then what was needed was a theory of midwifery. This view held sway over Marx his entire life because, as he saw it, he offered not just another vision of the future but a completely new enterprise. The idea for a new enterprise can be found in the same September letter to Ruge, discussed earlier, following the comment about all the confusion surrounding the *whither*. He considers his new enterprise as qualitatively different from the utopians' enterprise because, as he writes to Ruge, "constructing the future and settling everything for all times are not our affair."[53] The new enterprise seeks not to "dogmatically anticipate the world" but rather to "find the new world through criticism of the old one."[54] Marx did not want to add to the confusion about the future by providing yet another system, but alternatively to decipher the path toward the future by focusing on the potentials in the present.

To do so, theoretical guidelines must be followed making "criticism of politics, participation in politics, and therefore *real* struggles, the starting point of our criticism." Following such guidelines would curtail the need to "confront the world in a doctrinaire way with a new principle: here is the truth, kneel down before it!" It would instead require the discovery of new principles for the world "out of the world's own principles." In doing so, Marx continues, "we do not say to the world: Cease your struggles, they are foolish; we will give you the true slogan of struggle. We merely show the world what it is really fighting for, and consciousness is something that it *has to* acquire, even if it does not want to."[55] Such a theoretical guide, moreover, avoids confronting the world with a ready-made system plucked out of the imagination which ignores both past development and present circumstances, and therefore leaping out of time. But most important, this new enterprise places a premium on understanding the real link between past, present, and future, without sacrificing the dreams of the past and their fulfillment in the future to the dark realities of the present. As Marx contemplates the unfolding of time he concludes that humanity "has long dreamed of possessing something of which it has only to be conscious in order to possess it in reality," and when correctly considering the relationship between the modes of time "it will become evident that it is not a question of drawing a great mental dividing line between past and future, but of *realizing* the thoughts of the past . . . it will become evident that mankind is not beginning a *new* work, but is consciously carrying into effect its old work."[56]

Of course Marx wrote this while still under the sway of the Left Hegelians, but it is quoted and interpreted here as that which is fundamental to all of his subsequent political thought—the idea of temporal coordination. In his famous eleventh thesis Marx protests against those philosophers who only *interpret* the world differently; the point, he says, is to *change* the world. But from his critique of the utopian socialists it is clear that the act of changing the world demands a specific interpretation of both change and the world. It demands an interpretation of past activity and its influence upon present activity, and it demands an interpretation of present activity toward future-potentials. It demands, in other words, an interpretation of human activity and its impact upon historical change. Suitably interpreted, as Marx concludes in an equally famous passage, "men make their own history, but they do not make it just as they please in circumstances they choose for themselves; rather they make it in present circumstances, given and inherited."[57] What follows are the most important grounds upon which Marx bases this conclusion.

Rendering a Historical Past for Labor (or for the Laborer)

While in 1843 Marx may have considered the *whither* more of an obstacle than the *whence*, it is actually the *whence* that occupies his subsequent theoretical lifework—a work that includes outlining a materialist theory of history that provides a noble past for labor and promises a glorious future for the laborer. Yet Marx's interpretation of the past allows him to focus upon future-potentials that have been conditioned by the economic development of the past.[58] His interpretation of the past emerges largely through his consistent attacks upon idealism. Contrasting a materialist approach to the study of the past with an idealist one, Marx takes as his starting point human beings who, he says, are not to be "taken in some sort of imaginary isolation or fixed abstraction, but rather in their real, empirically observable process of development under definite conditions."[59] This basic materialist starting point considers human activity and the "material conditions of life, those in which [human beings] find themselves, as well as those which they have created through their own efforts," as necessary conditions for both the apprehension of history and the apprehension of its discernible trajectory.[60] As Marx sees it, once human activity is properly delineated "history ceases to be a collection of dead facts, as it is with abstract empiricists, or an imagined action of imagined subjects, as it is with the idealists."[61] To properly delineate the history of human activity the "physical organisation of these individuals and, arising out of this, their relationship to the rest of nature" must be established because as Marx argues "all historiography must proceed on the basis of these natural conditions and their modifications through the actions of men in the course of history."[62] Marx contends, moreover, that distinguishing humans from animals is not difficult and many have rightly distinguished the two by pointing to consciousness and religion; however, the list of distinguishing characteristics can get fairly long. What is most salient for Marx is that humans "begin to distinguish themselves from the animals as soon as they begin to *produce* their means of life, a step which is conditioned by their physical organization. In producing their means of life, they indirectly produce their material life itself."[63]

A similar contrast is made, albeit in decidedly abstruse language, in his *Paris Notebooks* where Marx posits that the "life of the species consists first of all, from the physical point of view, in the fact that man (like the animal) lives on inorganic nature" but the "more universal man is, compared to the animal, the more universal is the sphere of inorganic nature on which he lives."[64] This is fundamental for Marx because the distinctiveness of a species "lies in the form of its life-activity, and free conscious activity is the species character of man."[65] Or put slightly differently, the "animal and its life-activity are one and the same" while "man makes his life-activity the object of his will and of his consciousness."[66] This is to say that humans are distinct in that they are not bound by a particular life-activity, but are instead universalizing with regard to the objects of their life-activity. And since they are self-conscious, the life-activity of humans can be freely creative rather than bound by instincts. Animals also produce, but as Marx puts it they produce "only under the pressure of immediate physical need, whereas man produces when free of physical need and in fact truly produces only when free of such need."[67] It is this free conscious life-activity that distinguishes humans from animal life-activity, and it is "precisely by reason of that is he a species-being."[68] For Marx, the possibility for free conscious activity, or the possibility of producing beyond the sphere of physical need, can be considered the *distinguishing potential* of the human species.[69] This is a potential that not only conditions self-production—thereby conditioning the *making* of human history—but also provides a normative force to Marx's political philosophy. Moreover, this potential for free activity may be interpreted as an ontological a priori, but minimally it constitutes the condition for making history—making history in other words presupposes the free activity of humans, or else we are left with something (or someone) else making history, and this latter alternative Marx would reject outright. Since humans are capable of generation through concrete and conscious action, or *praxis*, they are capable of creating their own history and, by extension, their own destiny.

Human activity for Marx, or the laboring process, is more than just the reproduction of the material means for existence. Because it usually has been considered in this way, it has been considerably neglected in historical writings and in political philosophy before Marx. But labor for Marx is an elemental constituent of his theory of human history because it is in the "fashioning of the world of objects that man actually begins to affirm himself as a *species-being*," and because the products of labor are the "*objectification of man's species life*, an objectification in which he duplicates himself not only in consciousness, intellectually, but also in working, practical fashion, in actuality, and thus he contemplates himself in a world he has created."[70] Or again, as he similarly writes in *The German Ideology*, human activity must be considered more than the "reproduction of the physical existence of the individuals"; instead it must be considered this as well as a "distinctive form of activity of these individuals, a distinctive form of expressing their life, a distinctive *form of life* of those very individuals. As individuals express their life, so they are. What they are, therefore, coincides with their production, both *what* they produce and with *how* they produce. Thus, what individuals are depends on the material conditions of their production."[71] However, if humans do indeed have the potential to *freely* express their life through universal self-production, this potential has rarely been realized, if at all. Instead humans have produced under conditions of class domination and general exploitation. Self-production in freedom is impossible for the human species as a whole so long as they are alienated from the product and process of production, so long as they are alienated from that which makes them truly human. It is this alienation that removes humans from a position that would enable them to create their own destiny through free, self-conscious activity—humans are lost in time, so to speak, and must grasp their historical nature.

The problem of alienation is of course central to Marx's understanding of human history, and it is a problem that he appropriates from Hegel. Hegel's great accomplishment, according to Marx, is that he "grasps man's self-creation as a process, objectification as loss of objectivity, as alienation and the superseding of this alienation," and he therefore "grasps the essence of *labor* and comprehends objective man . . . as being the result of his *own labor*."[72] Marx praises Hegel's insight into the dialectics of the labor process—of objectification, alienation, and the overcoming of this alienation—because underlying this philosophical expression is the "*actual, active* relationship of man to himself as a species-being."[73] Marx argues, however, that "Hegel knows and acknowledges only labor of the abstractly spiritual kind," and therefore cannot possibly express the real experience of the material world.[74] Central to this critique of Hegel's conception of the labor process is the status of objectivity in Hegel's philosophy. Marx argues that when it comes down to the fundamental question of which comes first, mind or matter, Hegel puts mind first. Thus Hegel's system is standing on its head; and as a result, his idealist outlook leads to an incorrect conception of human beings, an incorrect conception of the objective world, and a faulty relation between the two.

Marx contends that Hegel sees human beings as essentially consciousness, and that consciousness is merely a moment in the life of Spirit. And since thought is the ultimate reality (central to idealism), then the world of objects is something inferior or merely a phenomenon of Spirit. By characterizing Hegel's thought in this way, Marx criticizes Hegel for conceptualizing labor as abstract mental labor, for conceptualizing the objective world as merely Spirit in its otherness (and therefore all objectification is self-alienation), and for concluding that the negation of this otherness can be accomplished at the level of philosophical reflection whereby alienation is overcome in thought and not in reality. Marx says that Hegel comes to this conclusion because for Hegel alienation is only the initial *intellectual* attitude that consciousness has toward the world, and a change in this intellectual attitude is all that is required to overcome this alienation. Alienation is overcome only in abstraction from the material world, in thought or in philosophy itself. Whereas Hegel describes the creation of the objective world as alienation of consciousness, as abstract thought to its objects, Marx contends that it actually describes the very practical self-production of human beings in the labor process. Real political and economic alienation are projected into pure thought—or into phases of consciousness that serve to mystify reality. By this Marx claims that Hegel pays little attention to the material world, and it is in this respect that real political and economic alienation, although presented clearly by Hegel, are projected into pure thought and never overcome in the material world: "therefore the criticism in the *Phenomenology* is concealed, mystifying and obscure to itself. Still, insofar as it does grasp man's *estrangement*—even though man appears in the guise of spirit alone—all elements of a criticism lie hidden within it, already *prepared* and *elaborated* in a way that often surpasses Hegel's own standpoint."[75]

To be fair to Hegel, though, when he speaks of the overcoming of alienation it is clear that he does not advocate an unworldly spiritual life—a return to an inner life or a recoiling from the *objective world*—for this was the path of the unhappy consciousness. For Hegel, overcoming alienation requires human activity to create an objective order that would satisfy the essential need for self-actualization in the world, which, in turn, would yield the condition for a reconciliation to this objective world. That is, humans express their essential being by creating objective institutions and coming to realize themselves objectively within these institutions. The objective world, therefore, is not annulled or degraded by Hegel as Marx seems to claim; the objective world is something wholly essential because the creation of objective institutions through human labor is necessary to express the essential being of humanity or to express the human spirit without which humans would be doomed to remain in the prison of subjectivity. In other words, for Hegel there is a reconciliation or an overcoming of alienation in practice—*in reality* and not just in thought. In certain respects, Hegel's *Phenomenology of Spirit*, the work to which Marx refers in the above quoted passage, discloses the totality which makes possible the mutual reconciliation of the subjective will with the existing objective order, the realization of the *Idea* of freedom or the *good* actualized.

Now it is true that Marx can raise a political objection here, and he certainly does. Marx claims that Hegel's idealism obscures the real (i.e., material) world of alienation, which in turn precludes a radical critique of alienation in the real world. A radical critique, according to Marx, would force one to recognize the need for the objective transformation of the world of alienation in order to overcome alienation. Marx argues that a true reconciliation involves establishing a completely different social universe, and that the existing conditions of political life must be abolished and replaced. Yet this is a different question. Marx is entitled to be dissatisfied with Hegel's solution, but in stressing the need for revolution in order to overcome alienation, it seems Marx *overstresses* Hegel's idealism to make his point. But looking past this exaggeration, the point still remains that the relationship between self-consciousness and estrangement, which is characteristic of Hegel's philosophy, is significant for Marx because a material being (natural being) with material powers works on real objects and in its alienation produces a real world of estrangement. Marx maintains that Hegel's speculative discovery of the origin of alienation and the speculative discovery of the movement of history—although obscure and mystifying—can be transposed into a practical theory for human liberation.[76] The transcendence—in practice—of alienated labor is the ultimate act of true human liberation.

The Course of History: Production and Temporality

With the fundamental materialist insight that "human beings must be in a position
to live in order to be able to make history," and that "man has a history because he
must *produce* his life," Marx submits a new way of looking at the past, and a new
way of conceptualizing historical development.[77] Marx certainly would not deny
that the past can be viewed from different standpoints.[78] For instance, he would not
deny that states, empires, art, ideas, and culture are all possible objects of study,
each with their own unique histories. Yet for Marx, understanding the *course of
historical development* requires a study of the laboring process and productive
activity *in* and *through* time. Marx had no doubt that his position was novel. He
complains that the Germans have "never had an *earthly* basis for history, and in
consequence have never had an historian," and while the French and English
"made the first attempts to give historiography a materialist basis in being the first
to write histories of civil society, of trade and industry," they made the mistake of
writing history "in a highly one-sided way, especially when they were captivated
by political ideology."[79] Marx concludes that previous accounts of history curiously
omit "this real basis of history," or in those rare cases when it is included, it is
regarded simply as a "secondary matter that stands outside the context of the
historical course of events."[80] History could only have been written, therefore,
ahistorically.[81] Even Hegel's philosophy of history is "nothing but the history of
philosophy." Instead of correctly understanding "history according to the order of
time," Hegel posits the "sequence of ideas in the understanding," thus erroneously
"constructing the world by the movement of thought," thereby "merely reconstructing systematically and classifying by the absolute method the thoughts which are
in the minds of all."[82]

Productive activity, Marx argues, is the "true *ground* of history,"[83] and to
understand productive activity in and through time is to unearth a major source of
historical change. But more to the point, when tracing productive activity across
time this historical change appears to follow a definite and progressive development. But this must not be attributed to some inherent quality in history itself.
Again, history according to Marx must not be construed as anything *but the history
of material production*: "History is nothing but the succession of individual
generations, each of which exploits the material, capital, and forces of production
bequeathed to it by all previous generations, and thus on the one hand continues the
traditional activity in greatly modified circumstances, and on the other hand
modifies the old conditions by a completely different activity."[84] Directly following
this account of history Marx warns the reader that "speculatively this can be
misinterpreted so as to make later history the goal of earlier history."[85] As an
example Marx uses the discovery of America, which is said to have actualized its
purpose in the French Revolution. "Thanks to this," Marx writes, "history is
assigned particular ends and becomes one 'person among other persons' . . .

whereas what is designated by the words 'destiny', 'purpose', 'germ', 'Idea' of earlier history, is nothing more than an abstraction of later history, an abstraction of precisely that active influence which earlier history exercises on later history."[86]

From a materialist standpoint the past exerts an active influence on later history because the specific historical conditions within which humans produce are historical products of past production. Human history, while characterized by Marx as nothing but the activity of humans pursuing aims, exhibits a *definite and progressive development* if only because the aims pursued are *always* circumscribed by past human activity, thereby giving history both a temporal coherence—past, present, and future are connected via productive activity—and, when viewed from the vantage point of the *immediate present*, an unmistakable historical trajectory. The latter would seem to follow if later history *is not misinterpreted* as the goal of earlier history. Abstractly, the historical past might appear to have a definite trajectory, but this is not an a priori necessary trajectory—it is only necessary when viewed as the historical development of present-day capitalist society. Bertell Ollman calls this aspect of Marx's theory of history "studying history backward."[87] It is important to realize, as Ollman interprets Marx's historical studies, that "searching for the preconditions of our capitalist present is the little appreciated key with which Marx opens up the past." Since Marx begins "with an already existing result, he is concerned to uncover what did in fact determine it, what the events themselves have transformed into its necessary preconditions. It is the necessity of the *fait accompli*, and only graspable retrospectively." What Ollman appropriately concludes, therefore, is that "necessity read backward into the past is of an altogether different order than the necessity that begins in the past and follows a predetermined path into the future."[88]

This relationship between the active influence of the past and historical development is summarized in *The German Ideology* when he writes that "at every stage of history there is a material result, a sum of productive forces," and this sum of productive forces is after all "an historically created relationship with nature and among individuals, *which every generation receives from its predecessor*," and it is "a mass of productive forces, of capitals [*Kapitalien*], and of circumstances that are, to be sure, on the one hand modified by the new generation but on the other *prescribe its own conditions of life and give it a definite development*, a specific character."[89] This is echoed numerous times throughout several of Marx's works, and all are more or less variations of the famous passage quoted earlier: "men make their own history, but they do not make it just as they please in circumstances they choose for themselves; rather they make it in present circumstances, given and inherited." The most explicit exposition of this perspective is in a letter from Marx to Annenkov, dated December 1846. In this letter Marx criticizes Proudhon for his ignorance of historical development.[90] While explaining to Annenkov his theory of historical development, Marx considers the role of productive forces in the shaping of human society, when he writes that "needless to say, man is not free to choose *his productive forces*—upon which his whole history is based—for every productive force is an acquired force, the product of previous activity." To be sure, the productive forces are products of human activity; however, this activity is "in turn circumscribed by the conditions in which man is placed by the productive forces already acquired, by the form of society which exists before him, which he does not create, which is the product of the preceding generation."[91] The fact that humans both *inherit* material conditions and *create* their own conditions is for Marx the secret to understanding the relation between past, present, and future.

From this it is apparent that according to Marx an important thread running through history is the productive forces of human activity which connect the past to the present in such a way as to allow history to be viewed as a composite whole. As Marx sees it, the "simple fact that every succeeding generation finds productive forces acquired by the preceding generation and which serve it as the raw material of further production, engenders a relatedness [*conexité*] in the history of man"; in other words, it "engenders a *history of mankind*."[92] For Marx every present is more or less the sum total (both quantitative and qualitative) of past productive forces. The past does not *dominate* the present but every present is nevertheless *prescribed* by its immediate past. Not only does this thread connect the present to a specific past (viewed a posteriori) but it likewise connects the present to a delimited future. While the accumulated past in the present does constrict present-possibilities, it never removes the possibility of creating something entirely new—in fact, the human potential for free activity which is central to Marx's anthropology presupposes the ability to create something entirely new. Besides, Marx's critical accounts of past and present forms of social, economic, and political life are not intended to simply interpret the world, but to assist in changing such forms of life.[93]

It could be stated, therefore, that what utopian thought has not understood hitherto is that humans are free to make history, but just not as they please or ex nihilo. Of course, in attempting to change the world the past may appear to dominate by weighing "like a nightmare on the brain of the living."[94] But this is why Marx proposes that those who wish to change the world must "let the dead bury the dead," and create their poetry not from the past but from the future instead.[95] The weight of the past would be, as it were, counterweighted by the poetry of the future, and this poetry must include a combination of utopian yearnings and hope.

The *Kairos* of the Modern Present

At times it appears that Marx is constructing a *universal* theory of historical development, with universal laws of development that apply in all cases; however, in a reply to an article by Nicolai K. Mikhailovski—though we should be willing to concede that this reply may be a reappraisal of his life work in his later years—Marx makes it clear that this was never his intention:

He [Mikhailovski] must by all means transform my historical sketch of the development of capitalism in Western Europe into a historical-philosophical theory of universal development predetermined by fate for all nations, whatever their historic circumstances in which they find themselves may be. . . . But I beg his pardon. That [view] does me at the same time too much honor and too much insult. . . . Thus events of a striking analogy, because they took place in a different historic milieu, led to entirely different results. If one studies each of these developments by itself and compares with each other, one will easily find the key to each phenomenon, but one would never thereby attain a universal key to a general historical-philosophical theory, whose greatest advantage lies in its being beyond history.[96]

What must be emphasized here is that Marx concerns himself with not just any present but instead the historically specific *present* of modern Western European capitalism—its *past* development and its possible *future* transformation are what interest him. By considering productive activity in and through time, Marx uncovers and gives an account of the discernible changes in the modes of production, each of which are designated by him as unique and epochal.[97] Moreover, while casting a studied glance upon the historical development of the productive forces of Western European capitalism, Marx focuses on, as he puts it at the beginning of the *Manifesto*, the indisputable fact that the "history of all hitherto existing society is the history of class struggles."[98] Now, if from a materialist standpoint productive activity is the true ground of history, then class struggle has been the true motive force of historical development. When tracing productive activity in and through time, history, Marx writes in one of the most sweeping and unadorned lines in political rhetoric, is exposed as a record of class struggles: "freeman and slave, patrician and plebeian, lord and serf, guild master and journeyman, in short, oppressor and oppressed stood in continual conflict with one another, conducting an unbroken, now hidden, now open struggle, a struggle that finished each time with a revolutionary transformation of society as a whole, or with the common ruin of the contending classes."[99]

The modern capitalist present is a product of this historical process. It is the result of past class struggles. It, too, is presently animated by class struggle—*unbroken, now hidden, now open struggle*—and, it too, according to Marx, will be transformed by subsequent class struggle. Marx argues, however, that an essential difference exists between the class struggle that is taking shape in the modern world and class struggles of times past; to wit, the modern present is on the threshold of true human emancipation. To transform that which has been inherited from the past requires a radical future-orientation to see the possible (not inevitable) developing in the womb of the present. Positioned between an inherited past filled with exploitation and human misery and a future that *could* inaugurate a process of true human history, the modern age is considered by Marx as nothing less than a propitious moment for decision and decisive action.

Marx views the capitalist present as only a phase in the historical development in the productive process of humanity, albeit a momentous one. Of course, from the standpoint of the bourgeoisie the past is considered as merely a prelude to the triumphant arrival of a full and unfettered market economy, and Marx would no doubt agree. When Marx writes in the *Manifesto* that the bourgeoisie has "obliterated all relations that were feudal, patriarchal, idyllic," and has severed all feudal ties between humans and replaced them with "naked self-interest, unfeeling hard cash," and has replaced "religious fervour," "zealous chivalry" and "philistine sentiment" with "egotistic calculation," and has substituted "exploitation cloaked by religious and political illusions" with "open, unashamed, direct, brutal exploitation," his depiction of the revolutionary role of the bourgeoisie is only in part ironic.[100] More important for Marx, however, is that "in scarcely one hundred years of class rule the bourgeoisie has created more massive and more colossal forces of production than have all the preceding generations put together."[101] For Marx, this is the truth of the modern world, but the question is who are to command these productive powers which, until the modern epoch, have "slumbered in the bosom of social labor."[102] The answer is contained in the secret of the nineteenth century, that is, in the emancipation of the working class. It is the modern working class, Marx argues, that shoulders the weight of past historical development, it is the modern working class which "represents, practically speaking, the complete abstraction of everything human," it is the modern working class whose living conditions "have reached the acme of inhumanity," and it is the modern working class who is slowly acquiring a "theoretical consciousness" and understands therewith that "it cannot liberate itself without destroying its own living conditions . . . without destroying *all* the inhuman living conditions of contemporary society which are concentrated in its own situation."[103]

However, the bourgeoisie would have the world believe that history, or at least economic history, has come to its final resting point, not the least because bourgeois economists consider capitalist relations and market forces as natural. What this means, according to Marx, is that capitalist relations are taken to be "themselves natural laws *independent of the influence of time*," which means, paradoxically, that "there has been history, but there is no longer any."[104] From his critical survey of past historical development, however, this conclusion is impossible for Marx to accept. As Marx sees it, "man never renounces what he has gained, but this does not mean that he never renounces the form of society in which he has acquired certain productive forces." The ways in which humans have produced, consumed, and exchanged have hitherto been *"transitory and historical."*[105] While the modern world has *gained* unprecedented powers of production, it also has inherited a society divided into opposing classes—the price paid for the historical development of these unprecedented productive powers. "Modern Bourgeois society," writes Marx, "which arose from the ruins of feudal society, has not transcended class conflict. It has merely established new classes, new conditions of oppression, new forms of struggle in place of the old."[106] The new struggle is but a new expression of that which has given past historical development its motive force, and will likewise give the present its motive force to enter into a future that could transcend class conflict—oppression and exploitation arising from class conflict has always given rise to the promise and hope for a better life, as authors of most utopian schemes will attest.

The promise that Marx's theory of historical development discovers in the womb of the modern present is the end to conflict and exploitation arising from class divisions, or, what is the same for Marx, the end of *prehistory*. Be assured, Marx declares, that the "bourgeois relations of production are the last antagonistic form of the social process of production—antagonistic not in the sense of individual antagonism but of an antagonism that emanates from the individuals' social conditions of existence—but the productive forces developing within bourgeois society create also the material conditions for a solution of this antagonism." As a result, "the prehistory of human society accordingly closes with this social formation."[107] While Marx does not discount the possibility of a peaceful transformation, he emphasizes that invariably "it is the bad side that produces the movement which makes history."[108] Either way, however, change must be revolutionary "because only in revolution can the *overthrowing* class successfully rid itself of all the old muck and become capable of giving society a new foundation."[109]

The future that the utopian socialists have envisaged can emerge from one final, as it were, apocalyptic clash between the classes. Just as the bourgeoisie had succeeded in its historical and revolutionary objective of liberating itself from feudal bonds and liberating economic production from the restraints of an outmoded feudal economic system by wresting control of the productive process, so, too, Marx argues, must the working class succeed in its historical and revolutionary objective of liberating itself from capitalist bonds and establishing a classless society where the productive process would be controlled collectively. To put an end to prehistory and to begin an epoch of true human history, the revolution must turn its back on the past, it must turn its back on the inheritance of class divisions, it must orient itself toward a future without classes, it must, in other words, jump over Rhodes. The future belongs to the laborer. Or more precisely, the future belongs to a society without class distinctions. This is the poetry, or poetic potential, of the future.

Notes

1. Göran Therborn, "Critical Theory and the Legacy of Twentieth-Century Marxism," in *The Blackwell Companion to Social Theory*, ed. Bryan S. Turner (Oxford: Blackwell Publishers, 1996), 54–55.

2. Therborn, "Critical Theory and the Legacy of Twentieth-Century Marxism," 55.

3. Marx, "Speech at the Anniversary of the *People's Paper*," in *Collected Works*, vol. 14 (New York: International Publishers, 1980), 655–56.

4. Marx, "Speech at the Anniversary of the *People's Paper*," 654. Robin Goodfellow (Puck) was a popular shape-shifting character from English folklore.

5. Marx, "Speech at the Anniversary of the *People's Paper*," 655.

6. Marx, "Speech at the Anniversary of the *People's Paper*," 655.

7. Marx, "The Eighteenth Brumaire of Louis Bonaparte," in *Marx: Later Political Writings*, ed. and trans. Terrell Carver (Cambridge: Cambridge University Press, 1996), 34.

8. Marx, "The Eighteenth Brumaire of Louis Bonaparte," 35. Hegel uses it in the preface to his *Philosophy of Right*, 11. The difference in emphasis is so obvious that the editor, Terrell Carver, could not resist adding his own bracketed comment: "There's no time like the present!"

9. Marx, "On Feuerbach," in *Marx: Early Political Writings*, ed. and trans. Joseph O'Malley (Cambridge: Cambridge University Press, 1994), 118.

10. Marx, "Letters from the *Deutsch-Französische Jahrbücher*," in *Collected Works*, vol. 3 (New York: International Publishers), 142.

11. Marx, "Letters from the *Deutsch-Französische Jahrbücher*," 142.

12. Marx, "Letters from the *Deutsch-Französische Jahrbücher*," 142.

13. If nothing else Marx understood the challenge facing a post-Enlightenment political philosophy that seeks to radically change the world.

14. Marx, "Letters from the *Deutsch-Französische Jahrbücher*," 142.

15. Frank E. Manuel and Fritzie P. Manuel, *Utopian Thought in the Western World* (Cambridge, Mass.: Harvard University Press, 1979), 701.

16. Locating their utopias in distant islands is not just a convenient literary device. At the time of More's and Campanella's writing, sea captains were indeed venturing off into *new* and *unknown* worlds.

17. J. C. Davis, "Utopianism," in *The Cambridge History of Political Thought: 1450–1700*, ed. J. H. Burns and Mark Goldie (Cambridge: Cambridge University Press, 1991), 335.

18. Davis, "Utopianism," 355.

19. See especially Krishan Kumar's *Utopia & Anti-Utopia in Modern Times* (Oxford: Basil Blackwell, 1991), 38, and Manuel and Manuel's *Utopian Thought in the Western World*, 458–60.

20. Kumar, *Utopia & Anti-Utopia in Modern Times*, 39.

21. Henri Saint-Simon, *Selected Writings*, ed. and trans. Keith Taylor (New York: Holmes and Meier Publishers, 1975), 136.

22. Manuel and Manuel, *Utopian Thought in the Western World*, 581.

23. Keith Taylor, *The Political Ideas of the Utopian Socialists* (London: Frank Cass and Company, 1982), 1.

24. The following exposition of the third section of the *Manifesto* designates Marx as the author largely for stylistic reasons. Of course, no disrespect to Engels is intended. However, it could also be pointed out, as David McLellan puts it, that "notwithstanding the appearance of their two names on the title page and the persistent assumption about joint authorship, the actual writing of the *Communist Manifesto* was done exclusively by Marx." *Karl Marx: His Life and Thought* (New York: Harper & Row, 1973), 180.

25. Marx and Engels, "Manifesto of the Communist Party," in *Marx: Later Political Writings*, 21.

26. Marx and Engels, "Manifesto of the Communist Party," 21.

27. Marx and Engels, "Manifesto of the Communist Party," 21.

28. Marx and Engels, "Manifesto of the Communist Party," 23. Marx considers the reformer Simonde de Sismondi (1773–1842) as an exemplar of this vision. Elsewhere a similar reproach is leveled against Sismondi and others who "wish to return to the correct proportion of production, while preserving the present basis of society." Marx explains that such a position is untenable if only because to be consistent one "must also wish to bring back all the other conditions of industry of former times." Marx, "The Poverty of Philosophy," in *Collected Works*, vol. 6 (New York: International Publishers, 1976), 137.

29. Marx and Engels, "Manifesto of the Communist Party," 23.

30. Marx and Engels, "Manifesto of the Communist Party," 25 and 26.

31. Marx and Engels, "Manifesto of the Communist Party," 26.

32. Manuel and Manuel, *Utopian Thought in the Western World*, 701. If one Adds Cabet and Weiling to this list it is easy to see, as Keith Taylor points out, that during the 1830s and 1840s these five thinkers "were regarded as the representatives *par excellence* of the new movement." Taylor, *The Political Ideas of the Utopian Socialists*, vii. In fact, the draft of the *Manifesto* lists Owen, Cabet, Weitling, Fourier, St. Simon, and Babeuf as exemplars of critical socialists. Marx, "Draft Plan for Section III of the Manifesto of the Communist Party," in *Collected Works*, vol. 6, 576.

33. Marx and Engels, "Manifesto of the Communist Party," 28.

34. Marx and Engels, "Manifesto of the Communist Party," 27.

35. Marx and Engels, "Manifesto of the Communist Party," 27.

36. Marx, "Contribution to the Critique of Hegel's Philosophy of Law: Introduction," in *Collected Works*, vol. 3, 187.

37. Marx and Engels, "Manifesto of the Communist Party," 27.

38. Marx and Engels, "Manifesto of the Communist Party," 27.

39. Marx and Engels, "Manifesto of the Communist Party," 28.

40. Marx and Engels, "Manifesto of the Communist Party," 27.

41. Marx, "The Poverty of Philosophy," in *Collected Works*, vol. 6, 210.

42. Marx and Engels, "Manifesto of the Communist Party," 28.

43. "To the extent that the class struggle develops and takes shape, this fantastic transcendence of the class struggle, this fantastic attack on the class struggle, loses all practical worth, all theoretical justification." Marx and Engels, "Manifesto of the Communist Party," 28.

44. Marx and Engels, "Manifesto of the Communist Party," 28.

45. Marx and Engels, "Manifesto of the Communist Party," 28. Here Marx is alluding to the utopian system of his favorite whipping boy, Etienne Cabet.

46. Kumar, *Utopia & Anti-Utopia in Modern Times*, 51.

47. A point that Hal Draper rightly stresses to counter the "myth" that Marx "invented the term 'utopian socialism' merely as a contemptuous denunciation." *Karl Marx's Theory of Revolution, Volume IV: Critique of Other Socialisms* (New York: Monthly Review Press, 1990), 2.

48. Marx, "Letters from the *Deutsch-Französische Jahrbücher*," 142.

49. Marx, "Preface to the Second Edition of Capital—January 24, 1873," in *Capital*, trans. Samuel Moore and Edward Aveling (New York: Modern Library, 1906), 21.

50. "The Civil War in France," in *Marx: Later Political Writings*, 188. Of course, we cannot be sure that the working class did indeed *know* this, but it is clear that Marx understood the struggle in this way.

51. Draper, *Karl Marx's Theory of Revolution*, 19.

52. Vincent Geoghegan, *Utopianism & Marxism* (London: Methuen & Co., 1987), 28.

53. Marx, "Letters from the *Deutsch-Französische Jahrbücher*," 142.

54. Marx, "Letters from the *Deutsch-Französische Jahrbücher*," 142.

55. Marx, "Letters from the *Deutsch-Französische Jahrbücher*," 144.

56. Marx, "Letters from the *Deutsch-Französische Jahrbücher*," 144.

57. Marx, "The Eighteenth Brumaire of Louis Bonaparte," 32.

58. It must be said that reconstructing this interpretation is difficult because his theory of history is not located in any one text but instead scattered throughout many texts. Moreover, as McLellan points out, "he began many projects but . . . finished none of them." McLellan, *Karl Marx: His Life and Thought*, 40.

59. Marx, "The German Ideology," in *Marx: Early Political Writings*, 125.

60. Marx, "The German Ideology," 123 and 125.

61. Marx, "The German Ideology," 125.

62. Marx, "The German Ideology," 123.

63. Marx, "The German Ideology," 123.

64. Marx, "Paris Notebooks," in *Marx: Early Political Writings*, 74.

65. Marx, "Paris Notebooks," 75.

66. Marx, "Paris Notebooks," 75.

67. Marx, "Paris Notebooks," 76.

68. Marx, "Paris Notebooks," 75. The most succinct definition of species-being [*Gattungswesen*] that Marx provides is this: "first, that [man] has his own species, or specific nature, and the species of all other things as the object both of his practical action and of his theorizing; and second, (another way of saying the same thing), that he regards and comports himself as the actuality of the living species, i.e. as a *universal* and therefore free being." "Paris Notebooks," 74.

69. The view presented here is indebted to Professor Victor Wolfenstein.

70. Marx, "Paris Notebooks," 76.

71. Marx, "The German Ideology," 124. Human nature, therefore, if one could speak of human nature in a Marxist sense, cannot escape the vicissitudes of time because for Marx "by thus acting on the external world and changing it [the human being], at the same time changes his own nature. He develops his slumbering powers and compels them to act in obedience to his sway." Marx, *Capital*, 197–98.

72. Marx, "Paris Notebooks," 87.

73. Marx, "Paris Notebooks," 87.

74. Marx, "Paris Notebooks," 87.

75. Marx, "Paris Notebooks," 85.

76. This Marx explicitly states in the "Preface to the Second Edition of Capital—January 24, 1873," and it is worth quoting at length: "In its mystified form, dialectic became the fashion in Germany, because it seemed to transfigure and to glorify the existing state of things. In its rational form it is a scandal and abomination to bourgeoisdom and its doctrinaire professors, because it includes in its comprehension an affirmative recognition of the existing state of things, at the same time also, the recognition of the negation of that state, of its inevitable breaking up; because it regards every historically

developed social form as in fluid movement, and therefore takes into its account its transient nature not less than its momentary existence; because it lets nothing impose upon it, and is in its essence critical and revolutionary." *Capital*, 26.

77. Marx, "The German Ideology," 127 and 129.

78. Marx would deny, however, that his theory of the past is the key that unlocks all the details of history.

79. Marx, "The German Ideology," 127.

80. Marx, "The German Ideology," 138.

81. Marx, "The German Ideology," 138.

82. Marx, "The Poverty of Philosophy," in *Collected Works*, vol. 6, 165. The phrase "history according to the order of time" is P. J. Proudhon's (1809-65). Proudhon uses the phrase to underscore the difference between this kind of history-writing with his own (Hegelian) kind. Marx uses the phrase to criticize Hegel and, by extension, Proudhon.

83. Marx, "The German Ideology," 137.

84. Marx, "The German Ideology," 135. In his work "The Holy Family" Marx is unequivocal in regard to the *status* of history: "*History* does *nothing*; it possesses *no* wealth, it wages *no* battles. It is man, real, living man, who does all that, who possesses and fights;" history does not use "man as a means to achieve *its own aims*; history is *nothing but* the activity of man pursuing his aims." *Collected Works* (New York: International Publishers, 1975), Vol. 4, 93. This also means that for Marx history has no meaning outside of what humans attribute to it.

85. Marx, "The German Ideology," 135. My italics.

86. Marx, "The German Ideology," 135.

87. Bertell Ollman, *Dialectical Investigations* (New York: Routledge, 1993), 136. Eric Hobsbawm similarly writes that "in his mature works Marx deliberately studied history in reverse order, taking developed capitalism as his starting point." Hobsbawm, "Marx and History," in *On History* (London: Abacus Books, 1998), 209.

88. Ollman, *Dialectical Investigations*, 136–38.

89. Marx, "The German Ideology," 137. My italics.

90. Marx, "Marx to Pavel Vasilyevich Annenkov," in *Collected Works*, vol. 38 (New York: International Publishers, 1982), 96.

91. Marx, "Marx to Pavel Vasilyevich Annenkov," 96.

92. Marx, "Marx to Pavel Vasilyevich Annenkov," 96. My italics. The original letter is written in French (see "Karl Marx–Friedrich Engels Briefwechsel—Mai 1846 bis Dezember 1848," in *MEGA*, Part III, vol. 2, 70–80), and the oddly coined word *conexité* is translated in the *Collected Works* as *relatedness*. However, *conexité* is translated perhaps better as *connectedness*.

93. "Criticism has torn up the imaginary flowers from the chain not so that man shall wear the unadorned, bleak chain but so that he will shake off the chain and pluck the living flower." Marx, "Contribution to the Critique of Hegel's Philosophy of Law," 176.

94. Marx, "The Eighteenth Brumaire of Louis Bonaparte," 32. Additionally, Marx writes elsewhere that "history is thorough and goes through many phases when carrying an old form to the grave." The last phase, according to Marx, is comedy, so as to allow humanity to "part with its past cheerfully." Marx, "Contribution to the Critique of Hegel's Philosophy of Law," 179.

95. Marx, "The Eighteenth Brumaire of Louis Bonaparte," 34.

96. Marx, *The Letters of Karl Marx*, ed. and trans. Saul K. Padover (Englewood Cliffs, N. J.: Prentice-Hall, 1979), 321–22.

97. Considered in the most general sense, therefore, the "Asiatic, ancient, feudal and modern bourgeois modes of production may be *designated* as epochs marking progress in the economic development of society." Marx, Preface to "A Contribution to the Critique of Political Economy," in *Collected Works*, vol. 29 (New York: International Publishers, 1987), 263. My italics.

98. Marx and Engels, "Manifesto of the Communist Party," 1.

99. Marx and Engels, "Manifesto of the Communist Party," 1–2.

100. Marx and Engels, "Manifesto of the Communist Party," 2–3.

101. Marx and Engels, "Manifesto of the Communist Party," 5–6.

102. Marx and Engels, "Manifesto of the Communist Party," 6.

103. Marx, "The Holy Family," 36–37.

104. Marx, "The Poverty of Philosophy," 174. My italics.

105. Marx, "Marx to Pavel Vasilyevich Annenkov," 96–97.

106. Marx and Engels, "Manifesto of the Communist Party," 2.

107. Marx, Preface to "A Contribution to the Critique of Political Economy," 264.

108. Marx, "The Poverty of Philosophy," 174. Marx specifically refers to England, the United States, and possibly Holland as countries where a peaceful transformation may be possible. See Marx, "On the Hague Congress," in *Collected Works*, vol. 23 (New York: International Publishers, 1988), 255.

109. Marx, "German Ideology," 181.

Chapter Five

Dawn and Decline

Modernity and Its Rapport with the Future

Each of the three preceding chapters deals with a semiautonomous moment in the early stage of modernity—a stage during which an increasingly disjunctive past and future testify to the breakup of a premodern temporality, and to the emergence of a specifically modern one. We have seen how prior to the divergence of past and future, temporality was predicated largely on repeatable cycles, eschatology, and espccially on tradition, where "in the scales of time," writes Anthony Giddens, "the side of the 'past' is much more heavily weighted down than that of the 'future.'"[1] The scale shifted with the advent of modernity. As the past lost its grip upon the future, a new horizon of expectations was opened. New schools of thought reassessed and even eliminated elements of a past now seen as supersedable and a present now seen at best as provisional. With the experiential continuity of the past thus weakened, history was formulated as a process of discrete events which allowed the future to be considered as distinct from, and better than, the past. Moreover, human history now could be considered as part of a continuing forward-moving process that allowed expectations to extend beyond what previous experience had offered. This gave great confidence to a writer like Condorcet who assures his readers that the human race will never again relapse into its ancient barbarity, and that nature has fixed no limits on human hopes and progress because the "real advantages that should result from this progress, of which we can entertain a hope that is almost certain, can have no other term than that of the absolute perfection of the human race."[2] From across the Atlantic Thomas Paine could similarly tell the readers of *Common Sense* that "we have it in our power to begin the world over again" and that "the birthday of a new world is at hand."[3] Such strident convictions could only emerge with a modern rapport with the future.

However, the divergence of past and future created an urgently felt need for new narratives connecting these modes of time. Temporal coordination became a sometimes explicit, sometimes implicit *problem* for modernity. While Kant, Hegel, and Marx address more or less three modern paradigms—enlightenment, idealism, and materialism—they were not featured in this study primarily because of this; they were instead chosen because they are major political philosophers situated at the epicenter of the temporal disruption ushered in with the birth of modernity. Shock waves were sent out from this epicenter and penetrated both the past, in the form of reinterpretations of its role and significance, and especially the future, in the form of new expectations. Positioned at this epicenter, all three thinkers propose the means to reconnect the past with the future by *recasting the significance* of the past and the future for the modern present. All three thinkers acknowledge and encourage the diminishing role of the past upon the present, and, to a greater or lesser extent, they help to unshackle future expectations from a strict reliance on past experience.

In this regard, we found Kant giving expression to the *Zeitalter der Aufklärung*, an age which often used the idea of light to characterize its philosophical projects. Whether it be the "radiant light of the sun" shining on the overcast sky of Europe, or the "*lumières de la raison*" providing humanity with genuinely useful knowledge, the idea of supplying a new light to guide the European world into a new future is a central feature of enlightened philosophical endeavors.[4] Kant expresses this new ethos most powerfully. In his *Idea of a Universal History*, we observed that the past can be viewed as a slow maturation of a hidden plan of nature to bring about progressive development through individual antagonism which, in turn, allows for the emergence of something new.[5] Progress had advanced generationally, he argued, as one generation provided a foundation for subsequent progressive advances. Hence, progress entails a single time line of development from one generation to the next, and without the idea of progress, so he tells us, such advancements would have been too difficult to discern in the darkness of the past. The idea of progress exposes the initially hidden plan of nature, which, in turn, reduces the past to a mere principle while at the same time increasing an awareness of how our own rational and constructive efforts could hasten a better future for our descendants. So while progress is only an idea of reason, it is nonetheless a very powerful if not a radical idea. According to Kant, it not only brings together into a single, unified, and universal whole what would otherwise be a planless aggregate of past human actions, but it also detours those who would wish to return to that which has been progressively superseded. In addition, as progress serves as a theoretical guidepost leading us into a better future, it gives humanity the confidence to become more future-oriented. Kant is adamant that now that the secret of the past has been revealed, humanity, or, more precisely, governments, must view progress as a regulative idea and thus consciously direct future history accordingly. In the past, a naturally induced teleology pushed humanity from behind, as it were, but now with imagination and vision humanity is pulled forward by the enchanting *idea* of progress.

To his credit, Kant did not presume to have had thoroughly examined the past in light of his theory of progress. He specifically said that he was leaving this task to others. Hegel and Marx did indeed examine the past more thoroughly, and both presented a modern conception of the future as that which is immanent in the process of history. Hegel consciously refrains from predicting or prescribing the future, while Marx disdains ready-made systems for future implementation. Even so, the modern problem of future orientation involves more than mere prophesying: while a future orientation need not predict the course of events, it nevertheless requires the ability to assimilate new experiences which cannot be easily explained or understood from previous experience. As we have seen, both Hegel's and Marx's philosophical programs can be interpreted at the very least as systematic attempts to make sense of the new, which was rapidly proliferating, while at the same time providing a vision that would make this new less obscure. The world has a purpose which reveals itself to the dialectician which, in turn, must be revealed to the world in order for it to be recognized, as we saw with Hegel, or revealed in order for it to be realized, as we saw with Marx.

Hegel was not satisfied with the enlighteners' war against the past—especially when coupled with the idea of an infinite improvement—and he offers a peaceful settlement to this war by recasting the past in a larger universe. It is one thing to argue, as did some enlighteners, that the past cannot provide *political* guidance, and quite another to seek actively to cut humanity off from the past and start anew armed only with abstract ideas fabricated by reason. While he is wary of the overly optimistic aspects of the Enlightenment, he is likewise wary of those who wish for a return to past political and social structures. Hegel revisits the past from the height of philosophical speculation and explores the destructive and creative dynamic of historical time in order to connect the present to a past denuded of its exemplarity. He constructs a way of capturing the change taking place in the modern world by observing a continuity within historical change and formulating an organizing principle appropriate to it. Historical change, according to Hegel, is a process whereby the idea of freedom is particularized into the material world as it moves through its various phases of development, thus becoming part of historical time and suffering the same fate as all things temporal. The demise of one particular phase, however, gives rise to yet another phase, bringing with it *new* social and political structures that coincide with its development. Moreover, as we have seen, this progressive development is not a simple advancement or improvement *over* the past, in the sense of eliminating this or that negative or irrational aspect of the past; it is instead an integration of that which is past within the present. Rather than view progress as a regulative idea as does Kant, Hegel sees the idea of freedom developing *in* history. The truth of the past is embedded in the present, and the historical specificity, or the integument within which this truth has developed, can be relegated to historical memory. Unlike Kant, however, who, with his regulative idea of progress requires future-oriented political action, the present is as far as Hegel's philosophy can take the modern world—though for him this is far enough. The task is left to Marx to turn Hegel's understanding of historical time into a call for action.

Hegel reengages the past from an idealist perspective, thereby hoping to provide a deeper philosophical understanding of historical development which could then help clarify the role played by the modern present within this development. Marx on the other hand reengages the past from a materialist perspective, thereby hoping not just to provide an understanding of the modern present but to radicalize it as well. As we have seen, Marx respects Hegel's teaching on historical time and criticizes the utopian socialists for their atemporal theoretical approaches to social, political, and economic change; Marx, however, is less timid than is Hegel about using the dialectical method to decipher a path into the future. Marx, like Kant, views the modern present as a time for future-oriented action. But whereas Kant expresses the optimistic ideals and desires of an enlightened age, Marx expresses the desperate reality and demands of an industrialized age. The past is viewed by Marx as a historical succession of productive forces and relations, or, what is the same, as a historical succession of class cleavages and exploitative relations. As a result, the modern present is forced to face its inherited past, and through one final revolutionary class struggle, it must cast off inhuman qualities in order to advance into human ones. Marx puts forward the idea that humanity stands at the frontier of true human history; however, this future cannot begin until capitalism is dismantled and class divisions become a relic of the past. As Marx sees it, all future enlightened projects are dwarfed by comparison.

Subtended by their attempts to reestablish temporal continuity, the chapters on Kant, Hegel, and Marx help us to understand better that which became a *special* problem for modernity. Temporal discontinuity is coterminous with modernity. Reestablishing temporal continuity with an emphasis on the future is not a flight of fancy; it is a maneuver that is indispensable for the maintenance of modern temporality and, therefore, modernity itself. To be sure, employing light from the future instead of the past has the advantage of both reestablishing temporal continuity and admitting that which the past could not: new expectations and possibilities for a better life. But this advantage is both a blessing and a curse for modernity. Maintaining temporal coordination through an orientation toward the future has proven to be difficult. It is easy to see that when the burden of past experiences was lifted off the shoulders of the present, a new burden was placed on the future. A past full of changeless change gave way to the awareness of historical change, an awareness of history as a series of discrete events, not as a movement away from, but as a movement toward, some ideal condition. Modernity was to obtain its legitimacy not from what it *is* but from what it is yet *to become*. Modernity, in other words, is consecrated not *by* time but consecrated *in* time.[6] But whereas the past in premodernity provided light for thousands of years, the future in modernity yielded a flash that was as bright as it was brief.

Storm from Paradise

Those near the epicenter witnessed a new world emerging and thought it could be better than the past. Humanity could leave the past behind. Many had reservations, and some even extolled the opposite. In this regard, Edmund Burke is a most fascinating representative. He is fascinating less because of what he believes is gained by deferring to past experiences and practices, than because of what he deems is lost when we fail to, or simply cannot, do so. Burke, who may be seen as a different kind of *onlooker* than the one praised by Kant, laments Europe's extinguished glory following the sweeping changes taking place around him. He, too, thinks that the French Revolution is an astonishing and unprecedented event: "It looks to me as if I were in a great crisis, not of the affairs of France alone, but of all Europe, perhaps even more than Europe. All circumstances taken together, the French revolution is the most astonishing that has hitherto happened in the world."[7] Yet unlike Kant, who reads into the revolution all that is splendid about the age of enlightenment—a genuine historical sign of an unbounded future—Burke looks upon it as a catastrophe. How could it be viewed otherwise when the revolutionaries are in the process of recklessly tearing down an edifice shaped by the collective wisdom of countless generations, and when they are arrogantly proposing to begin anew by remolding the social fabric according to the personal and selfish whims of the enlighteners? The radically new expectations unleashed by the pledge of liberty and the promise of equality strike Burke as specious if not as altogether unnatural. Not based upon the solid ground of past experience and inheritance, the pledge of liberty is but a fanciful metaphysical abstraction; and the promise of equality is but a pernicious modern fiction. Unlike any other political event in historical memory, the French Revolution for Burke represents a conscious and perhaps irreparable rift between the past and present, and, worse, a rift that may not be containable within France itself.

Horrified by what this entails for future generations, which will now inherit ruins rather than a home, but more concerned with the destruction of the past, Burke becomes eulogistic. Gone forever are "all the pleasing illusions which made power gentle and obedience liberal, which harmonized the different shades of life, and which by a bland assimilation incorporated into politics the sentiments which beautify and soften private society." Pleasing or not, these illusions have been cruelly dispersed by the "new conquering empire of light and reason." Burke could hardly believe that those who deem themselves masters of the present rather than mere "temporary possessors" think that "all the decent drapery of life is to be rudely torn off" and that "all the superadded ideas, furnished from the wardrobe of a moral imagination, which the heart owns and the understanding ratifies, as necessary to cover the defects of our naked, shivering nature, and to raise it to dignity in our own estimation, are to be exploded, as a ridiculous, absurd, and antiquated fashion."[8] Even with mounting evidence to the contrary, Burke still held the position that nothing fundamentally new can be discovered.[9] If reforms be necessary, these should be considered only insofar as they conserve.[10] This is what the revolutionaries fail to understand, and their ignorance will be a plague upon future generations. Humanity must be persistently mindful of that which an established tradition offers if only because "when ancient opinions and rules of life are taken away, the loss cannot be estimated. From that moment we have no compass to govern us; nor can we know distinctly to what port we steer."[11] If, Burke argues, we continually allow ourselves to be seduced by the "floating fancies or fashions" of the modern age, which seem only to glorify the relentless pursuit of that which is new, "the whole chain and continuity of the commonwealth would be broken; no one generation could link with the other; men would become little better than the flies of a summer."[12] *Unbounded* future indeed.

However much Burke looks to be swimming against the unrelenting current of historical change, there is an important truth at the core of his position. The conceit of the modern age, if it could be put this way, is the belief that humanity could sever itself from the past, from centuries that gave political and spiritual nourishment to the present, without experiencing profound consequences, some obvious and some not so obvious. And even though the past was to be replaced by a new and better future, Burke warns us that the future alone can offer little nourishment for humanity. Those who wish to anchor humanity in the future, he says, will soon find that "their humanity is at their horizon,—and, like the horizon, it always flies before them."[13] This insight, written at the beginning of the modern journey away from the past and toward the future, is as profound as it is prescient. However, while Burke may place the blame on the enlighteners for severing humanity from the past, this is only partially accurate. Severing, of course, has an active quality to it. What Burke does not want to see is that the past, as a coherent tradition, had been disintegrating appreciably before the enlighteners came onto the European stage and, moreover, it was less of a foe than perhaps even they had realized. The past was vulnerable to enlightened attacks because, since at least the late Middle Ages, a confluence of fundamental changes had been taking place in religion, in society, in political institutions, in scientific knowledge, and in the economies of Europe which made it less possible to hold up the past as exemplary, or, at least made it difficult to believe that the future had nothing new to offer that the past had not already experienced.

It is hard not to think, moreover, that Burke's insistence *on* tradition corresponds to a problem *of* tradition itself: tradition could no longer *seamlessly* connect past, present, and future and, as a consequence, an essential part of tradition was undermined. If the past ceased to throw its light upon the future, as Tocqueville so aptly put it, then there is no better illustration of this than with the past embedded within a tradition. Besides, it was not long after Burke that tradition became but one voice of the past among many. Tradition is but a singular way of interpreting, of organizing, and of hierarchizing the past, and as the eighteenth century turned into the nineteenth, many interpretations of the past were posed.

Burke often chastised those in power who lacked an understanding of the historical past. But the past was no longer *Burke's past* once the study of history, for example, a budding academic discipline by the 1830s, came into its own. The nineteenth century is often considered the golden age of historiography, and with good reason. Breisach reminds us that "as the quest for knowing the meaning of the multitude of often puzzling events grew, people relied on historians to find explanations for the many changes as well as the assurance of continuity and stability in the midst of change."[14] Political philosophers were not alone, therefore, in their quest to reestablish temporal continuity by reinterpreting the past. What is more, historians often became "counselors of rulers, guides for political parties, and articulators of the *Volksgeist*," and in doing so "historians did not quite replace the philosophers and theologians but in many ways they surpassed them in influence, as the educated became used to calling on historiography to interpret human life, or at least to aid in approaching most problems historically."[15] Fortified with new methods and new concerns, historians plundered the past to such a degree that Nietzsche, in the last quarter of the nineteenth century, saw fit to express complaints about the surfeit of history. "All of us," writes Nietzsche, "suffer from a debilitating historical fever."[16] Whether debilitating or not, the important point is that the road modernity left behind became more foreign and less recognizable.

If nineteenth-century historiography helped to alter the way in which the past was viewed—if only by the sheer volume of material that was, and still is, unearthed—then so, too, did the late nineteenth century discovery of psychoanalysis. With Freud's retrospective theory of mental processes—the significance of which can only be hinted at here—the *past* returns with a vengeance.[17] Psychoanalysis provides a startling view of the persistence of the past, according to which early phases of individual mental development are preserved and exist "alongside of the final form." Or, to be more precise, "what is past in mental life *may* be preserved and is not *necessarily* destroyed" and, therefore, "it is rather the rule rather than the exception for the past to be preserved in mental life."[18] While Kant tells us that humanity has finally reached the stage of maturity—thus leaving the immature past behind—Freud tells us about how much of our past (immaturity) we actually bring with us as we move through history. The past is not just preserved, it is also active and actively influences adult behavior. The past that is preserved in the form of memories, which are stored in the preconscious, is less interesting here than is the past that is preserved in the form of unconscious demands for instinctual gratification, which "dominates the operation of the mental apparatus from the start."[19] The unconscious is the "oldest" province of the mind and "contains everything that is inherited, that is present at birth."[20] To speak of its preservation may not be completely correct, since the unconscious knows no time; put more correctly, the future will always be encroached upon by a *timeless* force. Because unconscious desires dominate our mental apparatus, and because the uninhibited satisfaction of desires runs counter to "all the regulations of the universe,"[21] an ineradicable or an *eternal* part of the human condition, according to Freud, is the psychic clash between the pleasure principle and the reality principle, or, put in a different context, between the desires of the unconscious and the dictates of civilization. This aspect of human history can no more be transcended than it can be easily or even harmlessly forgotten. Promises of a totally *new* and grand future are little more than fantasies. Freud's theory does not completely preclude the possibility of improvement in the future, but it does set limits on the possible. At any rate, to escape unhappiness and to survive suffering is probably the best the future can offer.[22]

Even though Freud's position regarding the persistence of the past has little in common with Burke's position, it nevertheless testifies that the past had become ever more complicated. But so, too, did the future, especially if we consider that the future of those who stood at the epicenter of modernity is now our past and, indeed, our present. Our own time, in other words, is the past's future. While the modern world's passage into the future has had mixed results, it is difficult to deny that the initial hope and anticipation for a radically new future have given way to the reality that the road upon which the modern world travels into the future is at best a *cul-de-sac*, and at worst a *new kind of barbarism*. The latter position is even held by obvious partisans of the cause of modernity. "From the beginning," Herbert Marcuse observes in his supplementary epilogue to *Reason and Revolution*, "the idea and reality of Reason in the modern period contained the elements which endangered its promise of a free and fulfilled existence: the enslavement of man by his own productivity; the glorification of delayed satisfaction; the repressive mastery of nature in man and outside; the development of human potentialities within the framework of domination."[23] Marcuse's colleagues, moreover, charge that the "Enlightenment has always aimed at liberating men from fear and establishing their sovereignty. Yet fully enlightened earth radiates disaster triumphant."[24] With quantification and calculation valorized and privileged as truth, and with the values of rational calculation in the service of profit, consumption, and individual material advancement, the social progress of the modern world, Max Horkheimer and Theodor Adorno argue, has produced unprecedented material wealth, material advancement and power, but only by replacing the substantive values of objective reason with a formal instrumental rationality, and only at the cost of the individual's devaluation relative to the economic powers. Assessing and reflecting upon the horrors of the twentieth century—a century that raised hope with its technological advances, as it dashed ideals of true human liberation—led even these radical stalwarts to suspend the utopian motif in their critical theory.[25] For Horkheimer and Adorno, escaping what now could be considered the fate of the modern future is not so simple: "it is not the portrayal of reality as hell on earth but the slick challenge to break out of it that is suspect."[26]

Has the journey into a better future been but a slick challenge to break free from the bonds of hell on earth? It does appear that the further modernity has moved away from the epicenter of its commencement the more hope for a better future has become intermixed with fear, a fear of a future that now seems more vast, unknowable, and uncertain than ever imagined. What has been experienced is certainly not what was expected, and what was expected has rarely been experienced. As the constancy of experience has given way to the uncertainties of anticipation, there is undoubtedly a sense that not only are we losing sight of a better future but, more ominously, that the journey of modernity has come to an end, leaving humanity marooned. Even a cursory examination of recent trends in cultural, social, and political theory reveals a concerted inclination for *discontinuation* evidenced by the proliferation of *end-of-theories*—end of ideology, end of history, end of utopia, end of philosophy, end of socialism, end of metanarratives, end of welfare capitalism, to name but a few—and by a pronounced uneasiness and uncertainty toward the future.

For instance, while considering the relation between history and the cultural forms in which it is perceived and articulated, Raymond Williams writes of a current dominant cultural form vaguely expressed as a loss of the future. This perception is a cultural tendency characterized by Williams as a widespread "loss of hope; the slowly settling loss of any acceptable future" with a concomitant "endless flow of colourful retrospect, simple idealizations of a happy and privileged past."[27] While Williams attributes this loss of the future to a dying social order entering what he calls a tragic dimension, David Harvey holds the view that the loss of the future stems from the sociocultural effects of a transition from Fordism to flexible accumulation. According to Harvey, the flexible motion of capital, characteristic of a post-Fordist economy, accentuates the ephemeral and fleeting in modern life and emphasizes the need for short-term planning, instantaneous adaptability to market fluctuations, and the cultivation of short-term economic gains.[28] The necessity to accommodate the demands of a constantly accelerating turnover rate in production and consumption has engendered, Harvey argues, "the loss of a sense of the future except and insofar as the future can be discounted into the present."[29]

Similarly concerned with this apparent loss of the future, Jürgen Habermas traces its cause to the eclipse of a particular type of utopian energy that has "lost its point of reference in reality."[30] The particular utopia which has seemingly come to an end, writes Habermas, is the one that places the potential of social labor at its core. The image of society based on social labor has inspired many European social movements, but none were as successful, or so successfully implemented, as the project of a social welfare state. Depicted both as a project that pacifies class antagonism endemic to capitalist growth through the use of democratically elected state power, and as a project that attempts to humanize labor conditions and to compensate for the indiscriminate violence of an unregulated market, the welfare state project, Habermas claims, has reached an impasse. As a project that embodies remnants of a utopia of social labor, the welfare state "has lost its persuasive power" and is "losing its power to project future possibilities for a collectively better and less threatened way of life."[31] The result has been both a contraction of the horizon of the future and the evacuation of future orientation in favor of a generalized sense of bewilderment.[32]

While Habermas would have us believe that it is *only* the utopian energy of social labor which has collapsed, Andreas Huyssen contends instead that it is the modern future-oriented utopia *as such* which has reached an impasse. What would appear as a corresponding symptom of a general loss of the future is what Huyssen diagnoses as a temporal shift in utopian thought from future fulfillment to past origins. That is, what seems to have occurred is the transformation of temporality in utopian imagination and discourse from its futuristic anticipatory pole toward memory and the past: "utopia and the past rather than utopia and the year 2000—that is what moves much of the art and writing that embodies the utopian imagination in our age of an alleged posthistoire and post-utopia."[33] Indeed, such theoretical notions as posthistoire, postutopia, postmodernism and other designations of our lateness—illustrated by the obligatory use of the *post* prefix—have also inspired extreme distrust in prospective vision or the projecting of possible futures. This distrust is clearly buttressed by the fashionable assault on the modern in a series of attempts to delegitimize (rightly or wrongly) the *grands récits* of the modern age,[34] as well as by a concomitant attempt to summarily put an end to history itself. This latter claim, made stylish by Francis Fukuyama, tells us that we have reached the end of history—not because we have lost the capacity to move forward, but because history has reached its goal. Future alternatives to our technological societies overseen by the ideal model of liberal democracy are thereby theoretically unnecessary, and politically excluded.[35] To put it succinctly, the future has already arrived. Two decades before the millennium Jean Baudrillard, in his allusively titled essay, "The Year 2000 Has Already Happened," puts forward a slight variation on this theme. Indicative of the end of history, Baudrillard claims, is the "collective prescience of the end of the event and of the living time of history" where memory is required to "confront the absence of the future and of the glacial time which awaits us."[36] Immersed in this glacial time, the end of history denotes the end of any possible change, development, transformation, revolution, and especially any possible hope for a better life in the future. Instead Baudrillard may be suggesting that what stands before us, as Steven Best and Douglas Kellner interpret his essay, is "a new, futureless future in which no decisive event can await us, because all is finished, perfected, and doomed to infinite repetition."[37]

Of course, we could easily muster many examples to counter the modern view that the future is open and can be molded by deliberate future-oriented action. Every utopia has its counterdystopia; however, looking over our past—and if the above trends in political and cultural theory are any indications—we can discern a trajectory that begins with a cautious optimism about the future, and ends with an uneasy pessimism about the future, or, if you will, from a belief in the human ability to envision and construct a home worth living in, to the contraction not only of prospective vision as such but also of the very capacity for envisioning the possibility that things could be different from what they presently are. Taking into consideration the prevailing attitudes toward the future, it would be fair to conclude that the future has become a vexing issue for cultural, social, and political theory. Perhaps we could even concur with Barbara Adam who, in her recent study of theories of time, maintains that "our contemporary approach to the future has shifted from colonization to something resembling elimination."[38] At the very least we should be able to see the point of a piece of graffiti written on a Berlin house wall announcing that "the future is no longer what it used to be."[39]

To put it coldly with just a hint of hyperbole, as does Peter Sloterdijk, we live today with "cement cities, bureau-democracy, listlessness, endless mediocrity, administration of deplorable states of affairs, lamenting prattle about responsibility, miserly pessimism, and insipid ironies."[40] This is hardly the new life envisioned by and hoped for by even the less sanguine of the enlighteners. But we are tired, maybe even exhausted, with the thought that the better future is just up ahead—after the next economic upswing, or after the next election, or after the next raise in salary. What we seem to be left with is a sequence of failed attempts at creating a good future. And what is ironic is that the uncertainty that today clouds future prospects comes at a time when the last vestiges of traditional forms of sociability and futurity have recently succumbed to modern temporality. To the extent that modern temporality requires the future to provide meaning and sustenance to the present—to furnish for the modern age what the past furnished for the premodern age—it is hard to deny that if the future is not what it used to be, then neither is it what it was supposed to be.

Retreat from the Future?

Is the future *passé*? Should we, too, join the chorus of voices and add the prefix *post* to yet another modern paradigm? A *post*future orientation, perhaps. We began this study with Tocqueville's observation that the past no longer shined its light upon the future. We saw how light from the past was replaced by light emanating from the future, or rather from political theories that offered a new light to guide the modern world into the future. This light, however, has since dimmed considerably. A belief in progress (in whatever guise) as a serious concept of human development has long since become severely tarnished, while philosophies of history are routinely dismissed as totalizing and hegemonic. As for the fate of future-oriented utopias, they have had the misfortune of being placed in the vane of history because utopia, if we believe Henri Lefebvre's account, "postulated an end to history and to historical alienation. So history, stimulated by utopianism, killed utopia off."[41] Anti-utopianism is after all a boom industry. Clearly, history no longer seems to be on our side, and our journey into a newly wrought future has been like life for Macbeth—a tale told by an idiot, full of sound and fury, signifying nothing. Without light from either the past or the future we could even say, as does Ernst Bloch in a different context, that presently we live in the darkness of the lived moment.

Indeed, what appears to be taking place is that the weight that had originally shifted from the past to the future has now shifted from the future to the present. The structure of temporality, in other words, looks to be changing yet again. Or at least we can witness today some of the symptoms indicating such a change. Politically, we see, for example, what can only be described as the politics of diminished expectations, a brand of politics that has been accompanying the economics of diminishing returns—at least for the majority. It is becoming clear that the modern notion of *upward mobility* predicated on future-oriented itineraries, which serve to coordinate into a coherent sequential continuity the otherwise disparate aspects of the modern individual's life, and which had become the dominant future-oriented paradigm of the modern age, now seems a chimera in the current economic phase of *downsizing* and *multiple careers*. Moreover, the increasingly generalized phenomenon of replacing lifelong careers, or at least stable, predictable employment with temporary and sporadic contractual work has disabled all but short-term goals. But perhaps the short term is all we have time for. That is, if we trust Helga Nowotny's claim that we today live in an *extended present*, in a world where "accelerated innovation is beginning to devour the future" and where "problems which could formerly be deferred into the future reach into the present . . . [and] press for solutions which admittedly may not be on the agenda until tomorrow but demand to be dealt with today."[42]

Recalling Tocqueville's discussion with the American sailor, we could now say that while Tocqueville may have uncovered a guiding ethos of the modern world, even he could not have predicted the subsequent pace at which innovation would take place, a pace that now appears to be collapsing the future into the present. The immediate future is being crowded by the new which lasts but for a brief moment—long enough however to draw the immediate future into the present by colonizing it with objects that are doomed to quickly become obsolete. As Huyssen has observed, "the new is always already muted, for we know that it tends to include its own vanishing, the foreknowledge of its obsolescence in its very moment of appearance," and therefore the "time span of presence granted the new shrinks and moves toward the vanishing point."[43] What is at hand here is not so much that the new has become attenuated than that it has become exacerbated to the point that, paradoxically, the new is no longer new, and the future-oriented temporality with which it was once entwined is eroded instead of reinforced. When accelerated innovation and the quick rise and even quicker decay of fads, fashions, and technologies produce a momentum of change that appears as if static, the present can but be experienced as being dominated by the omnipresence of the same.[44] Such a state of affairs is less likely to foster a vision of the future that qualitatively defers from the present, and even less likely still to garner the strength to actively impinge upon the present in the name of a better and qualitatively different future. How can one imagine a future beyond the immediate present when, as Marc Augé points out, everything seems to occur today "as if there were no history other than the last forty-eight hours of news, as if each individual were drawing its motives, its words, from the inexhaustible stock of an unending history of the present?"[45]

If, as advertisements often tell us, the future is now, or if we simply do not have time for the future, it is clear that the present is having a hard time containing continual disappointments with modernity. One unsettling consequence of this can be seen in the current tendency toward regressive as opposed to future-oriented political projects—regressive projects embodied, for example, by fundamentalist, nationalist, and neo-ethnic movements. "With blithe lightness of mind," writes Michael Ignatieff, "we assumed that the world was moving irrevocably beyond nationalism, beyond tribalism, beyond the provincial confines of the identities inscribed in our passports, towards a global market culture which was to be our new home." Apparently we were just "whistling in the dark."[46] Seeking redemption in uncontaminated past origins, however, is less a return to the past than it is a politically contrived regression: "no longer based on any substantial experiences of a shared political destiny," Gopal Balakrishnan notes, "the longing for national identity becomes a taste for a pseudo-archaic ethnicity cranked out in made-to-order forms by the heritage industry."[47] So, while future orientation is incessantly blunted by the consequences of accelerated change, and while the containment and management of systemic bugs predominates over sustained political projects, and while ever increasing segments of the population are subjected to the exigencies of the short term, there are those who wish to take refuge in vague memories and more often than not, in newly invented pasts.

These are but a few of the symptoms of an apparent change in modern temporality, a change which, whether by necessity or by design, now accentuates the present over the future and, more increasingly, a newly invented past over both the present and the future. As we look upon ideas of progress, upon philosophies of history, and upon future-oriented utopias with a jaundiced eye, we lose that which gave the modern present a sense of direction, a sense of purpose, and a sense of destiny. As a result our present is becoming directionless, purposeless, and ever more dangerous. Temporality is being disrupted once again, and it is probably no coincidence that this disruption is taking place now that there is a shortage of long-term future-oriented projects—as we have seen, when the perspective of one mode of time is changed, the other modes are likewise changed. Those situated at the epicenter of the temporal disruption ushered in with the advent of modernity saw the need for temporal coordination, and perhaps we are witnessing today some of the effects of life in the modern world without it—we are becoming, as Burke had warned, little better than flies of a summer.

While our current rapport with the future could be a mere exaggerated cultural reaction to the end of the millennium, it could also be a symptom of a more profound sociocultural phenomenon. Whether at hand be a passing fad, a gradual erosion of the conditions for the possibility of thinking of the future, or an inevitable entropic exhaustion of future orientation, these are problems that should demand our attention. One thing is undeniable, if temporal disruption can be considered a consequence of modernity, then perhaps temporal coordination is more difficult a problem than was first believed. Perhaps coordinating temporality through a future orientation was already beset with problems which are only now coming into focus. The need to rethink temporal coordination, to rethink the connection between our past, our present, and our future, is a very real problem that we face today. However, it may be premature to declare a *post*future-oriented age. The irony of our current dilemma is that even if we could afford to dismiss an orientation toward the future, to do so would be to give up on the past, yet again. To reject a future orientation, in other words, would be to succumb to a typically modern impulse to reject the past, but only this time it is our modern past with its future orientation that would be rejected.

The journey thus far has been a treacherous one; however, we can ill afford to leap over our past into an even more distant one. Besides, there are no serviceable routes back. To use an admittedly overused phrase, we have already crossed the Rubicon—*alea iacta est*. In reestablishing temporal continuity—maybe with more respect for the road traveled and less naive optimism for the road yet traveled—we may find that we are today only halfway through our journey. And if we are having difficulty envisioning a livable future destination, then perhaps we need to sharpen our vision. In doing so, we might wish to keep in mind that "mankind and the world carry enough good future; no plan is itself good without this fundamental belief in it."[48]

Notes

1. Anthony Giddens, *The Consequences of Modernity* (Stanford, Calif.: Stanford University Press, 1990), 38.

2. Condorcet, *Sketch for a Historical Picture of the Progress of the Human Mind*, trans. June Barraclough (Westport, Conn.: Hyperion Press, 1991), 184.

3. Thomas Paine, *The Complete Writings of Thomas Paine*, vol. 1, ed. Philip S. Foner (New York: Citadel Press, 1945), 45.

4. Ulrich Im Hof, *The Enlightenment*, trans. William E. Yuill (Oxford: Blackwell, 1994), 4–7. This time period, of course, is considered the age of Enlightenment or *le siècle des lumières* or *i lumi* or *Aufklärung*, all of which express the idea of light or illumination.

5. As an aside, Alexander Chryssis points to a common motif in Kant, Hegel and Marx when he writes that "the concept of *cunning*, either in the form of 'cunning of nature' (Kant) or in the form of 'cunning of reason' (Hegel), was the cornerstone upon which the most eminent representatives of classical German philosophy grounded their own philosophical interpretations of history. . . . Marx and Engel's philosophy of history . . . is also inconceivable without a concept of cunning. In this case we may talk of the 'cunning of

production.'" Chyssis, "The Cunning of Production and the Proletarian Revolution in the *Communist Manifesto*," in *The Communist Manifesto: New Interpretations*, ed. Mark Cowling (Edinburgh: Edinburgh University Press, 1998), 97.

6. This is in contrast to a premodern view that M. I. Finley captures when he reminds us that "even kings claiming divine right were no less insistent (when they had some basis, however thin) on the long duration of their dynastic line: legitimacy *consecrated by time* was often a more powerful ideology than consecration by God in the face of competing dynastic claims or revolutionary threats." *Politics in the Ancient World* (Cambridge: Cambridge University Press, 1983), 133. My italics.

7. Edmund Burke, *Reflections on the Revolution in France* (Oxford: Oxford University Press, 1999), 10.

8. Burke, *Reflections*, 77.

9. In contrasting the intellectual current in England with that of France, Burke writes that "we are not the converts of Rousseau; we are not the disciples of Voltaire; Helvetius has made no progress amongst us. Atheists are not our preachers; madmen are not our lawgivers. We know that *we* have made no discoveries; and we think that no discoveries are to be made, in morality; nor many in the great principles of government, nor in the ideas of liberty, which were understood long before we were born."Burke, *Reflections*, 86.

10. "We must all obey the great law of change. It is the most powerful law of Nature, and the means perhaps of its conservation." "Letter to Sir Hercules Langrishe (1792)," in *The Philosophy of Edmund Burke: A Selection from His Speeches and Writings*, ed. Louis I. Bredvold and Ralph G. Ross (Ann Arbor: University of Michigan Press, 1960), 175.

11. Burke, *Reflections*, 78.

12. Burke, *Reflections*, 95.

13. Burke, "Letter to a Noble Lord (1798)," in Bredvold and Ross, *The Philosophy of Edmund Burke*, 233.

14. Ernst Breisach, *Historiography: Ancient, Medieval & Modern*, (Chicago: University of Chicago Press, 1994), 261.

15. Breisach, *Historiography: Ancient, Medieval & Modern*, 261–62.

16. Friedrich Nietzsche, "On the Utility and Liability of History for Life," in *Unfashionable Observations*, trans. Richard T. Gray (Stanford, Calif.: Stanford University Press, 1995), 86.

17. This study has consciously avoided the problem of experience and temporal coordination at the *individual* level. Psychoanalysis is mentioned in passing only because of its subsequent impact on twentieth-century political, social, and cultural thought.

18. Sigmund Freud, *Civilization and Its Discontents*, ed. and trans. James Strachey (New York: W. W. Norton & Company, 1961), 20. A good example of this is found in one of Freud's earliest published works where he considers the ancient belief that dreams give knowledge of the future. He responds by saying that "it would be truer to say instead that they give us knowledge of the past. For dreams are derived from the past in every sense." However, dreams do foretell the future in the sense that "by picturing our wishes fulfilled, dreams are after all leading us into the future. But this future, which the dreamer pictures as the present, has been moulded by his indestructible wish into a perfect likeness of the past." Freud, *The Interpretation of Dreams*, ed. and trans. James Strachey (New York: Avon, 1965), 660. The idea of returning to a past phase of development eventually leads Freud to conclude that "the aim of all life is death" and that human life can be viewed generally as a continual struggle between the *Lebenstrieb* (life-drive) and the *Todestrieb* (death-drive).

Beyond the Pleasure Principle, ed. and trans. James Strachey (New York: W. W. Norton & Company, 1961), 32.

19. Freud, *Civilization and Its Discontents*, 24.

20. Freud, *An Outline of Psychoanalysis*, ed. and trans. James Strachey (New York: W. W. Norton & Company, 1949), 2. If Freud, moreover, contends that political and religious history can be viewed as a series of attempts to reinstate the authority of the primal father, then we could concur with Richard Lichtman's claim that "as the past prevails, so the authority of the past prevails." *The Production of Desire* (New York: Free Press, 1982), 52.

21. Freud, *An Outline of Psychoanalysis*, 2.

22. Freud, *Civilization and Its Discontents*, 25.

23. Herbert Marcuse, *Reason and Revolution* (New York: Humanities Press, 1983), 433.

24. Max Horkheimer and Theodor W. Adorno, *Dialectic of Enlightenment*, trans. John Cumming (New York: Continuum Press, 1988), 3.

25. See Leo Lowenthal's "The Utopian Motif in Suspension," in *An Unmastered Past: The Autobiographical Reflections of Leo Lowenthal* (Berkeley: University of California Press, 1987).

26. Horkheimer and Adorno, *Dialectic of Enlightenment*, 256.

27. Raymond Williams, *The Politics of Modernism: Against the New Conformists* (London: Verso, 1989), 96–97.

28. David Harvey, *The Condition of Postmodernity* (Oxford: Blackwell, 1990), 286–87.

29. Harvey, *The Condition of Postmodernity*, 291.

30. Jürgen Habermas, "The Crisis of the Welfare State and the Exhaustion of Utopian Energies," in *Jürgen Habermas on Society and Politics: A Reader*, ed. Steven Seidman (Boston: Beacon, 1989), 288.

31. Habermas, "The Crisis of the Welfare State and the Exhaustion of Utopian Energies," in *Jürgen Habermas*, 288.

32. Habermas, "The Crisis of the Welfare State and the Exhaustion of Utopian Energies," in *Jürgen Habermas*, 286.

33. Andreas Huyssen, *Twilight Memories: Marking Time in a Culture of Amnesia*, (New York: Routledge, 1995), 88.

34. As Jean-François Lyotard writes, "the grand narrative has lost its credibility, regardless of what mode of unification it uses, regardless of whether it is a speculative narrative or a narrative of emancipation." *The Postmodern Condition: A Report on Knowledge*, trans. Geoff Bennington and Brian Massumi (Minneapolis: University of Minnesota Press, 1984), 37.

35. Francis Fukuyama, *The End of History and the Last Man* (New York: Free Press, 1992).

36. Jean Baudrillard, "The Year 2000 Has Already Happened," in *Body Invaders*, ed. Arthur and Marilouise Kroker (London: Macmillan Education, 1988), 43.

37. Steven Best and Douglas Kellner, *Postmodern Theory: Critical Interrogations* (New York: Guilford, 1991), 134.

38. Barbara Adam, *Time and Social Theory* (Cambridge, U. K.: Polity Press, 1990), 140.

39. Helga Nowotny, *Time: The Modern and Postmodern Experience*, trans. Neville Plaice (Cambridge, U. K.: Polity Press, 1994), 50.

40. Peter Sloterdijk, *Critique of Cynical Reason*, trans. Michael Eldred (Minneapolis: University of Minnesota Press, 1987), 385.

41. Henri Lefebvre, *Introduction to Modernity: Twelve Preludes, September 1959–May 1961*, trans. John Moore (London: Verso, 1995), 79.

42. Nowotny, *Time: The Modern and Postmodern Experience*, 11.

43. Huyssen, *Twilight Memories*, 26. Huyssen's observation is similar to Lefebvre's comment that "once, in an ahistorical society with virtually no conscious history, nothing began and nothing came to an end. Today everything comes to an end virtually as soon as it begins, and vanishes almost as soon as it appears." Lefebvre, *Introduction to Modernity: Twelve Preludes,* 165.

44. See Fredric Jameson's *The Seeds of Time* (New York: Columbia University, 1994), 17.

45. Marc Augé, *Non-Places: Introduction to an Anthropology of Supermodernity*, trans. John Howe (London: Verso, 1995), 104.

46. Michael Ignatieff, *Blood and Belonging: Journeys into the New Nationalism* (Toronto: Viking, 1993), 2.

47. Gopal Balakrishnan, "The National Imagination," *New Left Review* (May/June 1995), 68. This should remind us of Marx's comment that if history does occur twice, then the first time it occurs as tragedy and the second time as farce.

48. Ernst Bloch, *The Principle of Hope*, vol. 1, trans. Neville Plaice, Stephen Plaice, and Paul Knight (Cambridge, Mass.: MIT Press, 1986), 447.

Selected Bibliography

Adam, Barbara. *Time and Social Theory*. Cambridge, U.K.: Polity Press, 1990.

Anderson, M. S. *Europe in the Eighteenth Century: 1713–1783*. New York: Longman, 1987.

Aquinas, Thomas. *On Kingship*. Translated by G. B. Phelan. Toronto: Pontifical Institute of Medieval Studies, 1949.

Arendt, Hannah. *Between Past and Future*. New York: Penguin, 1993.

Aristotle. *The Politics*. Translated by Carnes Lord. Chicago: University of Chicago Press, 1984.

Auerbach, Erich. *Mimesis: The Representation of Reality in Western Literature*. Translated by Willard R. Trask. Princeton, N.J.: Princeton University Press, 1953.

———. *Scenes from the Drama of European Literature*. Minneapolis: University of Minnesota Press, 1984.

Augé, Marc. *Non-Places: Introduction to an Anthropology of Supermodernity*. Translated by John Howe. London: Verso, 1995.

Augustine, St. *The City of God*. Edited and translated by R. W. Dyson. Cambridge: Cambridge University Press, 1998.

———. *On Christian Teaching*. Translated by R. P. H. Green. Oxford: Oxford University Press, 1997.

Avineri, Shlomo. *Hegel's Theory of the Modern State*. Cambridge: Cambridge University Press, 1972.

Bacon, Francis. *Novum Organum*. Edited and translated by Peter Urbach and John Gibson. Chicago: Open Court, 1994.

Bakhtin, M. M. *The Dialogic Imagination: Four Essays*. Translated by Caryl Emerson. Edited and translated by Michael Holquist. Austin: University of Texas Press, 1981.

Balakrishnan, Gopal. "The National Imagination." *New Left Review* (May/June 1995).

Baudrillard, Jean. "The Year 2000 Has Already Happened." In *Body Invaders*. Edited by Arthur Kroker and Marilouise Kroker. London: Macmillan Education, 1988.

Becker, Carl. *Heavenly City of the Eighteenth-Century Philosophers*. New Haven, Conn.: Yale University Press, 1932.

Beiser, Frederick. *Enlightenment, Revolution & Romanticism: The Genesis of Modern German Political Thought: 1790–1800*. Cambridge, Mass.: Harvard University Press, 1992.

Berman, Harold J. *Law and Revolution: The Formation of the Western Legal Tradition*. Cambridge, Mass.: Harvard University Press, 1983.

Berman, Marshall. *All That Is Solid Melts into Air: The Experience of Modernity*. New York: Simon & Schuster, 1982.

Best, Steven, and Douglas Kellner. *Postmodern Theory: Critical Interrogations*. New York: Guilford, 1991.

Bloch, Ernst. *The Principle of Hope*. Translated by Neville Plaice, Stephen Plaice, and Paul Knight. Cambridge, Mass.: MIT Press, 1986.

Blumenberg, Hans. *The Legitimacy of the Modern Age*. Translated by Robert M. Wallace. Cambridge, Mass.: MIT Press, 1983.

Bolingbroke, Lord. *Historical Writings*. Edited by I. Kramnick. Chicago: University of Chicago Press, 1972.

Borst, Arno. *The Ordering of Time: From the Ancient Computus to the Modern Computer*. Translated by Andrew Winnard. Chicago: University of Chicago Press, 1993.

Bradley, A. C. "Aristotle's Conception of the State." In *A Companion to Aristotle's Politics*. Edited by David Keyt and Fred D. Miller Jr. Oxford: Blackwell, 1991.

Bredvold, Louis I., and Ralph G. Ross, eds. *The Philosophy of Edmund Burke: A Selection from His Speeches and Writings*. Ann Arbor: University of Michigan Press, 1960.

Breisach, Ernst. *Historiography: Ancient, Medieval & Modern*. Chicago: University of Chicago Press, 1994.

Bultmann, Rudolf Karl. *History and Eschatology*. Edinburgh: Edinburgh University Press, 1957.

Burke, Edmund, *Reflections on the Revolution in France*. Oxford: Oxford University Press, 1999.

Calinescu, Matei. *Five Faces of Modernity: Modernism, Avant-garde, Decadence, Kitsch, Postmodernism*. Durham, N.C.: Duke University Press, 1987.

Cassirer, Ernst. *The Philosophy of the Enlightenment*. Translated by Fritz C. A. Koelln and James P. Pettegrove. Princeton, N.J.: Princeton University Press, 1979.

Chryssis, Alexander. "The Cunning of Production and the Proletarian Revolution in the *Communist Manifesto*." In *The Communist Manifesto: New Interpretations*. Edited by Mark Cowling. Edinburgh: Edinburgh University Press, 1998.

Cieszkowski, August. "Prolegomena to Historiosophy." In *Selected Writings of August Cieszkowski*. Edited and translated by André Liebich. Cambridge: Cambridge University Press, 1979.

Cohen, Jean L., and Andrew Arato. *Civil Society and Political Theory*. Cambridge, Mass.: MIT Press, 1992.

Cohn, Norman. *The Pursuit of the Millennium: Revolutionary Millenarians and Mystical Anarchists of the Middle Ages*. London: Random House, 1970.

Condorcet, Jean-Antoine-Nicolas de Caritat. *Sketch for a Historical Picture of the Progress of the Human Mind*. Translated by June Barraclough. Westport, Conn.: Hyperion Press, 1991.

Connolly, William E. *Political Theory and Modernity*. Oxford: Basil Blackwell, 1988.

Coste, René. *Marxist Analysis and Christian Faith*. Translated by Roger A. Couture, OMI, and John C. Cort. New York: Orbis Books, 1985.

Cranston, Maurice. *Philosophers and Pamphleteers: Political Theorists of the Enlighten-ment.* Oxford: Oxford University Press, 1986.

Davis, J. C. "Utopianism." In *The Cambridge History of Political Thought: 1450–1700.* Edited by J. H. Burns and Mark Goldie. Cambridge: Cambridge University Press, 1991.

Diderot, Denis. "Encyclopedia." Translated by Stephen Gendzier. In *The Enlightenment: A Comprehensive Anthology.* Edited by Peter Gay. New York: Simon & Schuster, 1973.

Dohrn-van, Rossum Gerhard. *History of the Hour: Clocks and Modern Temporal Orders.* Translated by Thomas Dunlap. Chicago: University of Chicago Press, 1996.

Draper, Hal. *Karl Marx's Theory of Revolution, Volume IV: Critique of Other Socialisms.* New York: Monthly Review Press, 1990.

Dupré, Louis K. *Passage to Modernity: An Essay in the Hermeneutics of Nature and Culture.* New Haven, Conn.: Yale University Press, 1993.

Edelstein, Ludwig. *The Idea of Progress in Classical Antiquity.* Baltimore: Johns Hopkins University Press, 1967.

Erasmus, Desiderius. *Education of a Christian Prince.* Translated by Neil M. Cheshire and Michael J. Heath. Cambridge: Cambridge University Press, 1997.

Estes, James M. "Officium Principis Christiani: Erasmus and the Origins of the Protestant State Church." *Archive for Reformation History,* 1992.

Feuerbach, Ludwig. *Principles of the Philosophy of the Future.* Translated by Manfred Vogel. Indianapolis: Hackett, 1986.

Finley, M. I. *Politics in the Ancient World.* Cambridge: Cambridge University Press, 1983.

———. "Revolution in Antiquity." In *Revolution in History.* Edited by Roy Porter and Mikuláš Teich. Cambridge: Cambridge University Press, 1986.

———. *The Use and Abuse of History.* New York: Viking, 1975.

Fontenelle, Bernard Le Bovier de. "Digression on the Ancients and the Moderns." In *The Idea of Progress since the Renaissance.* Edited and translated by W. Warren Wagar. New York: John Wiley & Sons, 1969.

Forbes, Duncan. "Introduction." In *Lectures on the Philosophy of World History.* Cambridge: Cambridge University Press, 1995.

Freud, Sigmund. *Beyond the Pleasure Principle.* Edited and translated by James Strachey. New York: W. W. Norton & Company, 1961.

———. *Civilization and Its Discontents.* Edited and Translated by James Strachey. New York: W. W. Norton & Company, 1961.

———. *The Interpretation of Dreams.* Edited and Translated by James Strachey. New York: Avon, 1965.

———. *An Outline of Psychoanalysis.* Edited and translated by James Strachey. New York: W. W. Norton & Company, 1949.

Frisby, David. *Fragments of Modernity: Theories of Modernity in the Work of Simmel, Kracauer, and Benjamin.* Cambridge, Mass.: MIT Press, 1986.

Fukuyama, Francis. *The End of History and the Last Man.* New York: Free Press, 1992.

Gay, Peter. *The Enlightenment: A Comprehensive Anthology.* New York: Simon & Schuster, 1973.

———. *The Enlightenment: An Interpretation.* vol. 1. New York: W. W. Norton & Company, 1966.

———. *The Enlightenment: An Interpretation.* vol. 2 New York: W. W. Norton & Company, 1969.

Geoghegan, Vincent. *Utopianism & Marxism*. London: Methuen & Co., 1987.

Giddens, Anthony. *The Consequences of Modernity*. Stanford, Calif.: Stanford University Press, 1990.

———. *Modernity and Self-Identity: Self and Society in the Late Modern Age*. Stanford, Calif.: Stanford University Press, 1991.

Goldman, Lucian. *Immanuel Kant*. Translated by Robert Black. London: New Left Books, 1971.

Green, Garrett. "Modern Culture Comes of Age: Hamann versus Kant on the Root Metaphor of the Enlightenment." In *What Is Enlightenment? Eighteenth Century Answers and Twentieth Century Questions*. Edited by James Schmidt. Berkeley: University of California Press, 1996.

Habermas, Jürgen. *The Philosophical Discourse of Modernity: Twelve Lectures*. Translated by Frederick G. Lawrence. Cambridge, Mass.: MIT Press, 1987.

———. *The Structural Transformation of the Public Sphere: An Inquiry into a Category of Bourgeois Society*. Translated by Thomas Burger. Cambridge, Mass.: MIT Press, 1989.

Hampson, Norman. *The Enlightenment: An Evaluation of Its Assumptions, Attitudes and Values*. New York: Penguin, 1968.

Hardimon, Michael O. *Hegel's Social Philosophy: The Project of Reconciliation*. Cambridge: Cambridge University Press, 1994.

Harvey, David. *The Condition of Postmodernity: An Enquiry into the Origins of Cultural Change*. Oxford: Blackwell, 1990.

Hegel, Georg Wilhelm Friedrich. *Hegel's Lectures on the History of Philosophy*. Translated by E. S. Haldane and Frances H. Simson. London: Routledge & Kegan Paul, 1955.

———. *Lectures on the Philosophy of World History: Introduction*. Translated by H. B. Nisbet. Cambridge: Cambridge University Press, 1995.

———. *Phenomenology of Spirit*. Translated by A. V. Miller. Oxford: Oxford University Press, 1977.

———. *Philosophy of Right*. Translated by T. M. Knox. Oxford: Oxford University Press, 1967.

Hobbes, Thomas. *Leviathan*. Edited by C. B. Macpherson. New York: Penguin, 1968.

Hobsbawm, Eric. *On History*. London: Abacus Books, 1998.

Horkheimer, Max, and Theodor W. Adorno. *Dialectic of Enlightenment*. Translated by John Cumming. New York: Continuum Press, 1988.

Horowitz, Asher, and Gad Horowitz. *"Everywhere They Are in Chains": Political Theory from Rousseau to Marx*. Scarborough, Ont.: Nelson Canada, 1988.

Huyssen, Andreas. *Twilight Memories: Marking Time in a Culture of Amnesia*. New York: Routledge, 1995.

Ignatieff, Michael. *Blood and Belonging: Journeys into the New Nationalism*. Toronto: Viking, 1993.

Im Hof, Ulrich. *The Enlightenment*. Translated by William E. Yuill. Oxford: Blackwell, 1994.

Jameson, Fredric. *The Seeds of Time*. New York: Columbia University Press, 1994.

Jauss, Hans Robert. *Question and Answer: Forms of Dialogic Understanding*. Edited and translated by Michael Hays. Minneapolis: University of Minnesota Press, 1989.

Kant, Immanuel. "Conjectures on the Beginning of Human History." In *Kant: Political Writings*. Translated by H. B. Nisbet. Edited by Hans Reiss. Cambridge: Cambridge University Press, 1991.

———. "The Contest of Faculties." In *Kant: Political Writings*. Translated by H. B. Nisbet. Edited by Hans Reiss. Cambridge: Cambridge University Press, 1991.

———. *Critique of Pure Reason*. Translated by Norman Kemp Smith. London: MacMillan Press, 1993.

———. *Groundwork of the Metaphysic of Morals*. Translated by H. J. Paton. New York: Harper Torchbooks, 1964.

———. "Idea for a Universal History with a Cosmopolitan Purpose." In *Kant: Political Writings*. Translated by H. B. Nisbet. Edited by Hans Reiss. Cambridge: Cambridge University Press, 1991.

———. *Kant: Political Writings*. Translated by H. B. Nisbet. Edited by Hans Reiss. Cambridge: Cambridge University Press, 1991.

Kern, Stephen. *The Culture of Time and Space: 1880–1918*. Cambridge, Mass.: Harvard University Press, 1983.

Koselleck, Reinhart. *Futures Past: On the Semantics of Historical Time*. Translated by Keith Tribe. Cambridge, Mass.: MIT Press, 1985.

Kumar, Krishan. *Utopia & Anti-Utopia in Modern Times*. Oxford: Basil Blackwell, 1991.

Lambert, Malcolm. *Medieval Heresy: Popular Movements from the Gregorian Reform to the Reformation*. Oxford: Blackwell Publishers, 1992.

Lefebvre, Henri. *Introduction to Modernity: Twelve Preludes, September 1959–May 1961*. Translated by John Moore. London: Verso, 1995.

Lichtman, Richard. *The Production of Desire*. New York: Free Press, 1982.

Liebich, André. *Between Ideology and Utopia: The Politics and Philosophy of August Cieszkowski*. Dordrecht: Reidel, 1979.

———, ed. *Selected Writings of August Cieszkowski*. Cambridge: Cambridge University Press, 1979.

Locke, John. *Two Treatises of Government*. Edited by Peter Laslett. Cambridge: Cambridge University Press, 1963.

Lowe, Donald M. *History of Bourgeois Perception*. Chicago: University of Chicago Press, 1982.

Löwith, Karl. *Meaning in History*. Chicago: University of Chicago Press, 1970.

Luhmann, Niklas. *The Differentiation of Society*. Translated by Stephen Holmes and Charles Larmore. New York: Columbia University Press, 1982.

Lyotard, Jean-François. *The Postmodern Condition: A Report on Knowledge*. Translated by Geoff Bennington and Brian Massumi. Minneapolis: University of Minnesota Press, 1984.

Machiavelli, Niccolò. *The Portable Machiavelli*. Edited and translated by Peter Bondanella and Mark Musa. New York: Penguin, 1979.

———. *The Prince*. Translated by Harvey C. Mansfield. Chicago: University of Chicago Press, 1985.

Manuel, Frank E., and Fritzie P. Manuel. *Utopian Thought in the Western World*. Cambridge, Mass.: Harvard University Press, 1979.

Marcuse, Herbert. *Reason and Revolution*. New York: Humanities Press, 1983.

Markus, R. A. "The Latin Fathers." In *The Cambridge History of Medieval Thought c.350–c.1450*. Edited by J. H. Burns. Cambridge: Cambridge University Press, 1988.

Marsden, John. *Marxian and Christian Utopianism: Toward a Socialist Political Theology.* New York: Monthly Review Press, 1991.

Marx, Karl. *Capital.* Translated by Samuel Moore and Edward Aveling. New York: Modern Library, 1906.

――――. "The Civil War in France." In *Marx: Later Political Writings.* Edited and translated by Terrell Carver. Cambridge: Cambridge University Press, 1996.

――――. "Contribution to the Critique of Hegel's Philosophy of Law: Introduction." In *Collected Works.* vol. 3. New York: International Publishers, 1975.

――――. "A Contribution to the Critique of Political Economy." In *Collected Works.* vol. 29. New York: International Publishers, 1987.

――――. "Draft Plan for Section III of the Manifesto of the Communist Party." In *Collected Works.* vol. 6. New York: International Publishers, 1976.

――――. "The Eighteenth Brumaire of Louis Bonaparte." In *Marx: Later Political Writings.* Edited and translated by Terrell Carver. Cambridge: Cambridge University Press, 1996.

――――. "The German Ideology." In *Marx: Early Political Writings.* Edited and translated by Joseph O'Malley. Cambridge: Cambridge University Press, 1994.

――――. "The Holy Family." In *Collected Works, Vol. 4.* New York: International Publishers, 1975.

――――. "Letters from the *Deutsch-Französische Jahrbücher.*" In *Collected Works.* vol. 3. New York: International Publishers, 1975.

――――. "Marx to Pavel Vasilyevich Annenkov." In *Collected Works.* vol. 38. New York: International Publishers, 1982.

――――. "On Feuerbach." In *Marx: Early Political Writings.* Edited and translated by. Joseph O'Malley. Cambridge: Cambridge University Press, 1994.

――――. "On the Hague Congress." In *Collected Works.* vol. 23. New York: International Publishers, 1988.

――――. "Paris Notebooks." In *Marx: Early Political Writings.* Edited and translated by Joseph O'Malley. Cambridge: Cambridge University Press, 1994.

――――. "The Poverty of Philosophy." In *Collected Works.* vol. 6. New York: International Publishers, 1976.

――――. "Speech at the Anniversary of the *People's Paper.*" In *Collected Works.* vol. 14. New York: International Publishers, 1980.

Marx, Karl, and Frederick Engels. "Manifesto of the Communist Party." In *Marx: Later Political Writings.* Edited and translated by Terrell Carver. Cambridge: Cambridge University Press, 1996.

McLellan, David. *Karl Marx: His Life and Thought.* New York: Harper & Row, 1973.

Mulgan, R. G. *Aristotle's Political Theory.* Oxford: Oxford University Press, 1977.

Nederman, Cary J, and Kate Langdon Forhan. "Introduction." In *Medieval Political Theory: A Reader.* Edited by Cary J. Nederman and Kate Langdon Forhan. New York: Routledge, 1993.

Nicholson, Peter P. "Kant, Revolutions and History." In *Essays on Kant's Political Philosophy.* Edited by Howard Williams. Cardiff: University of Wales Press, 1992.

Nietzsche, Friedrich. "On the Utility and Liability of History for Life." In *Unfashionable Observations.* Translated by Richard T. Grey. Stanford, Calif.: Stanford University Press, 1995.

Nowotny, Helga. *Time: The Modern and Postmodern Experience.* Translated by Neville Plaice. Cambridge, U.K.: Polity Press, 1994.

O'Brien, George Dennis. *Hegel on Reason and History*. Chicago: University of Chicago Press, 1975.

Ollman, Bertell. *Dialectical Investigations*. New York: Routledge, 1993.

Osborne, Peter. *The Politics of Time: Modernity and the Avant-Garde*. London: Verso, 1995.

Padover, Saul K., ed. and trans. *The Letters of Karl Marx*. Upper Saddle River, N.J.: Prentice-Hall, 1979.

Paine, Thomas. "Common Sense." In *The Complete Writings of Thomas Paine*. vol. 1. Edited by Philip S. Foner. New York: Citadel Press, 1945.

Peperzak, Adriaan Th. *Philosophy and Politics: A Commentary on the Preface to Hegel's Philosophy of Right*. Dordrecht: Martinus Nijhoff, 1987.

Plato. *The Republic*. Translated by G. M. A. Grube. Indianapolis: Hackett, 1974.

Polansky, Ronald. "Aristotle on Political Change." In *A Companion to Aristotle's Politics*. Edited by David Keyt and Fred D. Miller Jr. Oxford: Blackwell Publishers, 1991.

Porter, Roy, and Mikulá Teich, eds. *Revolution in History*. Cambridge: Cambridge University Press, 1986.

Ricoeur, Paul. *Time and Narrative*. vol. 3. Translated by Kathleen Blamey and David Pellauer. Chicago: University of Chicago Press, 1988.

Riedel, Manfred. *Between Tradition and Revolution: The Hegelian Transformation of Political Philosophy*. Translated by Walter Wright. Cambridge: Cambridge University Press, 1984.

Rudé, George. *Europe in the Eighteenth Century: Aristocracy and the Bourgeois Challenge*. Cambridge, Mass.: Harvard University Press, 1972.

Saint-Simon, Henri. *Selected Writings*. Edited and translated by Keith Taylor. New York: Holmes and Meier Publishers, 1975.

Salisbury, John of. *Policraticus*. Translated by Cary J. Nederman. Cambridge: Cambridge University Press, 1996.

Saner, Hans. *Kant's Political Thought: Its Origins and Development*. Translated by E. B. Ashton. Chicago: University of Chicago Press, 1967.

Schmidt, James, ed. *What Is Enlightenment? Eighteenth Century Answers and Twentieth Century Questions*. Berkeley: University of California Press, 1996.

Schnädelbach, Herbert. *Philosophy in Germany: 1831–1933*. Translated by Eric Matthews. Cambridge: Cambridge University Press, 1984.

Seidman, Steven, ed. *Jürgen Habermas on Society and Politics: A Reader*. Boston: Beacon, 1989.

Sloterdijk, Peter. *Critique of Cynical Reason*. Translated by Michael Eldred. Minneapolis: University of Minnesota Press, 1987.

Solomon, Robert C. *In the Spirit of Hegel*. Oxford: Oxford University Press, 1983.

Taylor, Charles. *Hegel*. Cambridge: Cambridge University Press, 1975.

Taylor, Keith. *The Political Ideas of the Utopian Socialists*. London: Frank Cass and Company, 1982.

Therborn, Göran. "Critical Theory and the Legacy of Twentieth-Century Marxism." In *The Blackwell Companion to Social Theory*. Edited by Bryan S. Turner. Oxford: Blackwell Publishers, 1996.

Thompson, E. P. "Time, Work-Discipline, and Industrial Capitalism." *Past and Present*, no. 38 (1967): 56–97.

Thompson, J. B. *The Media and Modernity.* Stanford, Calif.: Stanford University Press, 1995.

Tocqueville, Alexis de. *Democracy in America.* Translated by Henry Reeve. Revised by Francis Bowen. New York: Vintage, 1945.

Toews, John Edward. *Hegelianism: The Path toward Dialectical Humanism, 1805–1841.* Cambridge: Cambridge University Press, 1980.

Wagar, W. Warren. "Modern Views of the Origins of the Idea of Progress." *Journal of the History of Ideas* 28 (January–March 1967): 55–70.

———, ed. *The Idea of Progress since the Renaissance.* New York: John Wiley & Sons, 1969.

Wagner, Peter. *A Sociology of Modernity: Liberty and Discipline.* New York: Routledge, 1994.

Weber, Eugene. *A Modern History of Europe.* New York: Norton & Co., 1971.

Wilkins, Burleigh Taylor. *Hegel's Philosophy of History.* Ithaca, N.Y.: Cornell University Press, 1974.

Williams, Howard, ed. *Essays on Kant's Political Philosophy.* Cardiff: University of Wales Press, 1992.

———. *Kant's Political Philosophy.* Oxford: Basil Blackwell, 1983.

Williams, Raymond. *The Politics of Modernism: Against the New Conformists.* London: Verso, 1989.

Index

About the Author

David Carvounas teaches political philosophy at the University of Toronto.